G000047927

GVLIELM CAMDEN · PRÆLECTVRÆ HISTORICÆ
CLARENT · FVNDATOR MVNIFIC ·

LONDINO NATVS DICIT

Hic oculos similesq vultus, hic ora tueri
Poteris, nec vltra hæc artifex quivit manus
ANNALES ipsum celebrisq BRITANNIA monstrant
Perenniora saxo et ære μνηματα.
Quisquis et Historiæ Cathedram hanc conscenderit esto
Benignitatis usque monumentum loquax.

DEGORÉ VS WHEAR PRIM
HISK TR. P. P. POSVYT

Marcus Ghæerardus pinxit

HISTORIÆ ECCE IVbar LVX Et præCLara VetVstæ CLarentIVs VIta seneX NONO NOVEMbris eXIIt

Soder del.   Engrav'd by James Basire 1749

CAMDEN'S BRITANNIA

SURREY
&
SUSSEX

From the edition of 1789 by Richard Gough

ANNOTATED AND EDITED BY
GORDON J. COPLEY

HUTCHINSON OF LONDON

Hutchinson & Co (Publishers) Ltd
3 Fitzroy Square, London W1

London Melbourne Sydney Auckland Wellington Johannesburg
and agencies throughout the world

First published 1977
This annotated edition © G. J. Copley 1977

Designed by Hans Schmoller R.D.I.
Set in Monotype Bembo

Printed in Great Britain by The Anchor Press Ltd,
Tiptree, Essex, on Smooth Wove 110 gsm paper supplied by
William Sommerville & Son Ltd, Croydon, Surrey
Bound by William Brendon & Son Ltd, Tiptree, Essex

ISBN 0 09 122000 9

To

Dr E. W. H. BRIAULT

splendid colleague and great 'chief'
for thirty-five years

BY THE SAME AUTHOR

The Conquest of Wessex in the Sixth Century
1954

An Archaeology of South-East England
1958

Names and Places
1964, revised edition 1972

English Place-Names and Their Origins
1968, revised edition 1971

Camden's Britannia: Kent
1977

CONTENTS

The maps of Surrey on pages 8–9 and Sussex on pages 40–41 are reproduced from
Gough's edition of *Camden's Britannia*

ILLUSTRATION SOURCES

William Camden (frontispiece), *Camden's Britannia*, edited by Richard Gough, 1789

SURREY

Chertsey Abbey, the Exchequer Ledger (p. 3): also reproduced in E. W. Brayley, *Topographical History of Surrey*, vol. 2, 1850, p. 175

Farnham Castle (p. 4), Waverley Abbey (p. 5), Croydon Church (p. 20): Francis Grose, *The Antiquities of England and Wales*, vol. 3, 1774

Guildford (p. 6), Croydon Palace (p. 19): Victoria and Albert Museum

The Palace of Oatlands (p. 7), Croydon, Archbishop Whitgift's Hospital (p. 20): Owen Manning, *The History and Antiquities of the County of Surrey*, vol. 2, 1809, facing pp. 786 and 553 respectively

Betchworth Castle (p. 12): J. Britton and B. Brayley, *The Beauties of England and Wales*, vol. 14, 1813, facing p. 159

Kingston Market Place (p. 13): *The Antiquarian Itinerary*, vol. 7, 1818

Richmond Palace (p. 15), Nonsuch Palace (p. 17), Wimbledon House (p. 21), Lambeth Palace (p. 22): British Museum

SUSSEX

Chichester Cathedral (p. 32), Old Shoreham (p. 46), Bramber Castle (p. 47), Pevensey Castle (p. 52): British Museum

Cowdray House (p. 42), Battle Abbey (p. 57), Hastings (p. 58), Bodiam Castle (p. 66): *The Beauties of England and Wales*, vol. 14, 1814, facing pp. 60, 180, 185, 201 respectively

Brighton (p. 48): T. W. Horsfield, *History and Antiquities and Topography of Sussex*, vol. 2, 1835, p. 119

Lewes Castle (p. 50): Francis Grose, *The Antiquities of England and Wales*, vol. 3, 1774

Herstmonceux Castle (p. 54): *The Antiquarian Itinerary*, vol. 1, 1815; Winchelsea (p. 62), Rye (p. 63): vol. 5, 1817

PREFACE

EVEN though Camden's *Britannia* is one of the more important starting-points in the study of local history, there has been only one edition of it since Gough's of 1789 and that is a splendid, though necessarily very expensive, facsimile of Bishop Gibson's edition of 1695, a work to be consulted in a well-stocked institutional library, but far beyond the means of most researchers. In recent decades, however, the number of students of local history has increased greatly and there is an ever-growing body of general readers who find pleasure and interest in the study of their own localities.

The present edition has been prepared with these students and readers in mind; yet even the scholar has been hampered in his work by the lack of an accessible and up-to-date edition of the *Britannia* that takes into account the vast increments in knowledge of the last two hundred years. He, too, has been kept in mind, though he is obviously free to reject everything in the following pages apart from Camden's text itself. Relevant to this is Gough's remark in his Preface: 'The want of an improved edition of the Britannia has been long complained of, and it is not perhaps easy to assign a reason why one has not been undertaken.' Of course, there are those who, from a position of superior scholarship, will regard the present work as a belated essay in effete antiquarianism. High in their ivory towers, they are unaware of the busy, unpretentious students who find deep satisfaction in exploring the local past and who have it well within their power to save at least a few scraps of worthwhile knowledge from oblivion. It is with them that the present editor unashamedly ranges himself, for without the work of these amateurs and more serious students, scholarship would be much the poorer.

The use of the translation of 1789 needs little defence. Richard Gough was a classical scholar and an antiquary in the great English tradition that goes back at least to William Worcester (1415–82). Moreover, Gough had the advantage of two earlier translations, Holland's of 1610 and Gibson's of 1695, the latter correcting the former at many points; and, inevitably in a work of such magnitude, Gough found a few errors of translation in Gibson and his collaborators, as well as of fact in the Camden original. Indeed, he corrects each of them about a dozen times in the chapters describing the five south-eastern counties. But even Gough, as he himself foresaw, is occasionally in error and without doubt this new edition will not be free of faults in spite of careful revisions.

It is, then, the translation made by Gough that is used in the following pages, for it is unlikely that Camden's Latin text could be better rendered. Gibson's and Gough's 'Additions' to their translations have not usually been reproduced for several reasons. Firstly, they contain much that Camden omitted, often deliberately; secondly, the growth of specialist studies has gone so far since 1789 that corrections would in total be more lengthy than the 'Additions' themselves; and, finally, they would have so enlarged the volume as to make it unwieldy in both content and format. Nevertheless, wherever Gough's comments illuminate Camden's text, they have been cited; and Gough's practice has been imitated in the reproduction of passages from the *Itinerary in England and Wales* . . . of John Leland wherever they are relevant to that text. In fact many passages from Leland are included which Gough did not reproduce, for almost always they either add interesting details or reveal the *Itinerary* as Camden's source.

The present editor's notes are intended to illuminate the text, bringing to bear on it the fruits of modern scholarship. As a scholar of the Renaissance, Camden believed in the unity of learning and he ranged widely over much of the field of contemporary knowledge. The modern reader would have the inconvenience of recourse to many works outside the category of historical topography if it were not for this edition. The sources cited in the notes will serve as pointers to the fuller clarification of Camden's text. Inevitably, the notes reflect this wide range of topics, sometimes giving them the appearance of an *omnium gatherum* of snippets; yet it must be said that there is much in the notes that has not been culled from books. Over several decades, and more intensively in recent years, the editor has visited the places described in the *Britannia*, some of them many times; and the visits have required much walking and the subsequent discarding of much mud.

Emphasis in the notes has constantly been put on those things that are still to be seen, some still as Camden saw them; and it is astonishing how much of what he described yet survives. Scratch the surface of twentieth-century suburbia and there is a good chance that a fragment of Tudor England will show through. Go out into the countryside or into the country towns and the survivals are numerous. The continuity from palaeolithic to medieval England that the editor sought to demonstrate in his *Archaeology of South-East England* needs no demonstration when comparisons are made between Camden's England and that 'pleasant land' of the later twentieth century, widely despoiled though it is by the 'developers'. For the barbarians and the wealthy philistines of Matthew Arnold's day are still with us and they have inordinate power. Camden's England is being bulldozed into oblivion faster than at any time in the past and almost all that is being newly provided is like a leprous disease on the fair face of the landscape. Hardly a town or village in southern England has been spared from some egregious defacement or other, whether it be electricity pylons, oil depots, refuse dumps, former establishments of Her Majesty's forces, new roads and factories, incongruous multi-storey office blocks or ordinary dwellings. Even the worst of what has been destroyed was better than almost all that has replaced it and vast profits have been indecently made at the expense of amenity. Yet it is something to be grateful for that generations of local worthies (some of them no doubt also despoilers in their time) and that national topographers such as Leland and Camden recorded what they did when they did.

Camden omits not a little that existed in his day and still exists, but generally speaking his omissions are not made good in the notes. On the other hand he includes much national history that the modern reader may be glad to ignore. Equally superfluous to any reader but a specialist are the lengthy passages of genealogy that break the thread of his narrative from time to time. But Camden knew well what he was doing. He was fully aware of the topics that would interest his literate contemporaries; and genealogy was certainly one of them.

The popularity of the *Britannia* is best attested by the number of times it was re-issued during his lifetime and soon after it. The first edition of 1586 was followed by a sixth as early as 1607; and Holland's translation of 1610 gave the work to a vastly greater number of readers. Five further editions in the original Latin had been published in Germany and Holland by 1662 as befitted the work of a scholar who was the correspondent of many of the most eminent European savants. Bishop Gibson's edition of 1695, with considerable additions to Camden's description of each county, was followed in 1722 by a further enlargement, reprinted in 1753 and 1772, the latter with minor corrections. Then came Gough, the greatest of the translators and editors.

The arrangement of the edition of 1789 is of some interest and requires description. The format was folio (17 × 10 inches) in three volumes, only the first of which is of present concern. John Nichols, the printer, was a friend of Gough and his companion on many of his travels. Nichols also wrote and published several works on historical topography.

The title-page is faced by a portrait of Camden engraved by James Basire from the original by Marcus Gheeraerts, painted in 1609 when the sitter was 58 years of age. The original is in the National Portrait Gallery. It had been presented by Camden to the History School at Oxford.

Following the title-page of the 1789 edition is a page of dedication by Gough to George III, 'Patron of Arts and Sciences, the Father of his People . . ., who has condescended to encourage researches into antiquity'. Gough's Preface comes next, with pagination v–viii. It includes two passages that are important for an understanding of his footnotes to Camden's text. In the present edition these notes appear at the foot of the text, lettered alphabetically. The new notes are numbered 01 to 99, 01 etc., and arranged in narrower columns. Gibson's and Gough's additions are not usually included.

The passages of Gough's Preface to be borne in mind are:

'All the bishop's [i.e. Gibson's] additions, distinguished by reference in Arabic numerals to his initial G. at the bottom of each page, are retained, except a very few, which were either uninteresting or erroneous, and most of them are enlarged and new modelled. A few mis-translations, instances of false English, trite observations, and false facts, are freely noticed at the bottom of the page.

'Even Holland's additions, though decried by Mr. Camden, are retained. Mr. Camden's marginal notes are marked by *, †, ‡. Among these must not be forgotten those marked *MS. n. Gale*, being made by the late Mr. Samuel Gale in the margin of his copy of the author's last edition, which has fallen into my hands.'

However, for *additions* in this passage read *notes* and for *Arabic numerals* read *letters of the alphabet*.

After Gough's *Preface* is placed the *Contents of the First Volume* and then follows 'The Life of Mr. Camden' by Gough, running to twenty-two folio pages (i–xxii), with extensive footnotes and specimens of the handwriting of Camden, Cotton and the French scholar Peiresc as a tailpiece.

The next page reproduces the title-page to the 1607 edition which was the original of Gough's translation:

BRITANNIA:

OR, A

CHOROGRAPHICAL DESCRIPTION

and so on as in the title-page to the 1789 edition; followed by Camden's dedication: 'To the most serene and most potent prince James, King of Great Britain, France, and Ireland; Defender of the Faith; born for the eternity of the British name and Empire; founder of lasting peace; author of public security; this work is dedicated by His Majesty's most devoted servant, William Camden'.

Mr. Camden's Preface to the Reader of three pages (i–iii) comes next. Then pp. iv–vii are taken up with Latin quotations, of which pp. v–vii are *Ad Lectorem*, 'To the Reader'. Page viii consists of twenty-six lines of Latin verse headed *Britannia*; and thereafter the real business of the book begins with the introductory chapters. In the present edition, which strictly follows the original spelling and punctuation, early forms of names are given in roman characters and appear in single quotes.

As may be seen from an earlier paragraph, Camden organized his material in rough conformity with the tribal divisions of Britain at the time of the Claudian conquest in A.D. 43, his information being derived from classical writers and not at all from archaeological writers, for none existed until at least two centuries later; and this is not inconsistent with Professor Douglas's statement (*English Scholars*, p. 25): 'His *Britannia* is essentially Roman Britain as seen in relation to its later growth.' Camden himself says that within the chapter devoted to each county he described as exactly as he could 'the bounds and qualities of soil, the places memorable in antiquity, the dukes, earls, barons, and the most antient and illustrious families; for it is impossible to mention them all'. His motive, like Leland's and Gough's, was 'the love of my country'. He claims to 'have omitted nothing that tended to discover the truth in matters of antiquity; to which purpose I have called in the assistance of a smattering of the antient British and Saxon languages. I have travelled over almost all England, and consulted the most experienced and learned persons in each county. I have carefully read over our own writers, and those among the Greek and Roman authors who made the least mention of Britain. I have consulted the public records, ecclesiastical registers, many libraries, the archives of cities and churches, monuments, and old deeds, and have made use of them as of irrefragable evidence, and when necessary quoted their very words however barbarous, that truth may have its full weight.'

In conclusion I would echo Gough's words from his *Preface* (p. viii): 'After all that has been, or can be, collected towards forming a complete edition of the BRITANNIA, much must be left to be corrected and supplied by attentive inspection of judicious travellers, or natives in the several counties. Increase of wealth renders property so fluctuating that it can hardly be ascertained for a succession of years.... Increase of cultivation makes rapid alterations in the face of the country. Old stations [sites] are levelled by the plough; old mansion-houses by modern refinement; and old titles revive in new families. Others may trace out many things barely hinted at here, and settle many points which are unavoidably left dubious.' Much of this is as true of the 1970s as it was of 1789.

Gough continues: 'The errors of former editors serve but to awaken a stronger apprehension in the present: and if the great author could not satisfy himself in his last and completest edition, what security is there for another editor's promise? If, in pointing out such errors, those of other Antiquaries are also animadverted on, this it is hoped is done with the candour due to respectable names.

'Far from presuming on an ability to correct the mistakes of preceding editors, it is not without the utmost diffidence I submit to the public eye the result of twenty years journeying, and a longer term of reading and enquiry.... I will not blush to acknowledge the secret satisfaction I feel in having attempted to publish a new edition of CAMDEN'S BRITANNIA.... I may hope there is some merit in uniting in one comprehensive view the various parts of BRITISH TOPOGRAPHY.'

The point of view of the twentieth-century editor could hardly be better expressed than by these words uttered as the French Revolution was smouldering into flame.

WILLIAM CAMDEN *was born in London in 1551, the son of a painter. Educated at Christ's Hospital and St Paul's School, he proceeded to Oxford in 1566, and it was on leaving the University in 1571 that he began his antiquarian travels. He was usher of Westminster School from 1575 to 1593, becoming its Headmaster in the latter year. Between 1578 and 1600 he continued his travels, but did so less extensively in later years. The first edition of the* BRITANNIA *appeared in 1586. He held the post of Clarencieux King of Arms from 1597 until his death in 1623.*

INTRODUCTION

ALMOST all that Camden undertook in the early and middle years of his life contributed towards the *Britannia* and he continued his studies right down to his last years with the purpose of correcting and amplifying it. His early years as a pupil at Christ's Hospital and at St Paul's School in London afforded him opportunities to become well acquainted with the City and Westminster and with their immediate neighbourhoods; and his five years as a student at Oxford (1566–71) enabled him to acquire knowledge of that very different part of the Thames Valley. We know from his Berkshire chapter (Gough edn, p. 148) that he made excursions to Wallingford at this time, and it is likely that he ventured in other directions as well. It was at Christ Church, Oxford, that he came to know Sir Philip Sidney, who encouraged him in his antiquarian investigations; and he continued them on his return to London in 1571, supplementing them by much journeying about the country.

His appointment as usher at Westminster School in 1575 and as Headmaster from 1593 to 1598 established him in a profession that maintained his classical scholarship in continuous active use, albeit at a lowly level in much of his teaching; and it gave him leisure even in term time to extend his reading and in vacations to make further excursions into the shires. In 1578 he had been in Norfolk and Suffolk and four years later he was again in Suffolk, continuing from there into Yorkshire and returning by way of Lancaster. He went into Devon in 1589, going as far west as Ilfracombe, where he held a prebend of Salisbury Cathedral; and in the following year he journeyed to Wales. He returned there in about 1593, going out by way of Salisbury and returning through

Oxford. In 1600 he went on an even more momentous journey to Carlisle in Cumberland, making a survey of the northern counties in the company of that other great Elizabethan antiquary, Sir Robert Bruce Cotton. The plague of 1603 caused him to take refuge at Cotton's country seat at Conington in Huntingdonshire, though it may well be that this was not the first visit to his friend's house.

John Aubrey (*Brief Lives*, ed. O. L. Dick, 1962, p. 150) preserved the memory of another of Camden's journeys into Wiltshire: 'When my grandfather went to schoole at Yatton-Keynell (neer Easton-Piers) Mr Camden came to see the church, and particularly tooke notice of a little painted-glasse-windowe in the chancell, which (ever since my remembrance) haz been walled-up, to save the parson the chardge of glazing it.'

Throughout his adult life he was probably exploring the counties nearest London. Even after the publication of the edition of 1607, Camden remained engrossed in amassing further material for the correction and enlargement of the *Britannia*. Gough recorded the fact that Thomas Hearne (d. 1735) had bequeathed to the Bodleian Library a copy of the 1607 edition 'with notes and emendations by Mr. Camden himself in the margin and on little pieces of paper fixed in their proper places'. And it was Aubrey, too, who recorded that Camden 'had bad Eies (I guesse Lippitude) which was a great inconvenience to an Antiquary'; and Aubrey's guess implies that the lippitude, which is soreness and blearedness, was the result of study, for he goes on: 'Mr Camden much studied the Welch language, and kept a Welsh servant to improve him in that language, for the better understanding of our Antiquities.'

But it was to more scholarly teachers, such as Lawrence Nowell (d. 1576), Lambarde (d. 1601), Joscelin (d. 1603) and Francis Tate (d. 1616), that he owed his knowledge of Old English. To Nowell, whose library he inherited, more than to the others, must go the credit for the new interest in Old English that developed in the 1560s and 1570s. He had produced a dictionary of Old English, still surviving in manuscript in the Bodleian Library. No such work of reference appeared in print before 1659; but it is most probable that Nowell's dictionary was in Camden's possession, at least from 1603. It was not only Camden who sat at Nowell's feet, for Archbishop Parker, Lambarde and Joscelin counted themselves his pupils in the years around 1565. Joscelin, too, compiled an Anglo-Saxon dictionary which, with other manuscripts and transcripts, were to pass into Cotton's collection where they were ready to Camden's hand. We know something of Cotton's loans to his antiquarian friends, to Bowyer, Agarde, Tate, Spelman and others in 1606; to Agarde, Tate and Camden in 1612, when Camden borrowed a collection of the lives of the saints (BM, Cotton Otho BX) and a 'Saxon Grammar that was Mr Gocelin' – which is further evidence that Camden continued his studies after 1607.

His appointment as Clarencieux King of Arms in 1597 was to be a cause of controversy with the jealous Ralph Brooke, York Herald, who no doubt believed he had more fitting experience for the post; and his venomous squib, *A Discoverie of certaine Errours . . . in the much commended Britannia 1594*, exposed mistakes in Camden's genealogical paragraphs which he acknowledged only ungraciously in the edition of 1600. But he had defenders even in the College of Arms itself, including Augustine Vincent who in reprisal attacked Brooke's *Catalogue of English kings, princes, and peers* of 1619. Yet the appointment as Clarencieux was probably intended to free Camden, now a well-loved and revered public figure, from the routine of a schoolmaster, so that in pursuance of his new duties he might travel the more.

Towards the end of his life, at any rate, he was employing deputies to make his visitations, for he was by then severely ill from time to time. But in his heyday these journeys would have enabled him to pursue his life's task with ease and without neglect of his official duties.

A further advantage of this appointment was that it brought him more frequently into the company of the other heralds, several of whom were enthusiastic antiquaries. The College of Arms of his time was a repository of antiquarian as well as of genealogical knowledge, readily put at Camden's disposal. In his Berkshire chapter (Gough edn, p. 152), he pays tribute to Robert Glover, Somerset Herald (d. 1588), as 'a person excellently well verst in the heraldic art'; and a little earlier he speaks of William Dethick, Garter King of Arms (d. 1612), as 'a person perfectly acquainted with all that relates to honor and nobility'. William Smith, Rouge Dragon (d. 1618), wrote *A Particular Description of England*, published in 1588, with town-profiles in colour, a picture of Stonehenge and a description of Cheshire with a bird's-eye view of Chester. Lastly, Sampson Lennard, Bluemantle Pursuivant (d. 1633), is characterized as 'a gentleman of singular virtue and politeness' in the Sussex chapter (Gough edn, p. 189). Clearly in these remarks Camden is repaying a debt of gratitude to his colleagues of the College.

The list of his friends includes many of the greatest minds of the Age. Sir Fulke Greville, Lord Brooke (d. 1628), a favourite of Elizabeth, was a patron and intimate friend whose influence with the Queen secured his place as a herald. To Sir Fulke was dedicated Camden's edition of the chronicles in 1603 and to him Camden bequeathed a piece of plate worth £10. Their friend in common, Sir Philip Sidney (d. 1586), already mentioned as a companion at Oxford, is paid far more than a conventional tribute in the account of Penshurst (Gough edn, p. 212). A third poet, Edmund Spenser (d. 1599), with strong antiquarian leanings, devoted to him a stanza of his *Ruines of Time*:

Camden the nourice [nurse] of antiquity
And lantern unto late succeeding age,
To see the light of simple verity,
Buried in ruins, through the great outrage
Of her own people, led with warlike rage.
Camden, though time all monuments obscure,
Yet thy just labours ever shall endure.

Ben Jonson, his pupil at Westminster School, poet and dramatist (d. 1637), wrote thus in heartfelt tribute to him:

Camden, most reverend head, to whom I owe
All that I am in arts, all that I know,
(How nothing's that?) to whom thy country owes
The great renown and name wherewith she goes;

and in dedicating to him the play *Every Man in his Humour* (1598) addressed him as 'the Most Learned, and My Honoured Friend Master Camden, Clarencieux'.

And there were many lesser men who had been his scholars, among them the bishops of London, Oxford, Durham, St Asaph and Rochester; but the greatest antiquarian of them all was his friend Sir Robert Bruce Cotton (d. 1631), whose library was open to Camden, Stow, Speed, Ussher and others with similar interests. It was to Cotton that Camden dedicated his *Remaines of a Greater Worke, Concerning Britain* of 1605, which consists of material collected with the *Britannia* in mind, but not included in it. The chapter headings are sufficient as an indication of its contents: Inhabitants, Languages, English Tongue, Christian Names, Surnames, Allusions, Rebus, Anagrams, Money, Apparel, Artillery, Armouries, Wise Speeches, Proverbs, Poems, Epigrams, Rhymes, Impresses [emblems], Epitaphs and Impossibilities. Cotton inherited the greater part of Camden's library.

Of an older generation, Lambarde (d. 1601) held several legal posts in London during the later part of his life when he could have been frequently in Camden's company. They had exchanged compliments in their major writings, Lambarde in his *Perambulation of Kent* (1570, edn of 1970, pp. 2–3) referring to 'Master Camden, the most

lightsome [elegant] antiquarie of this age'; and Camden returned the compliment, acknowledging his indebtedness to Lambarde in the introductory paragraph to his chapter on Kent (Gough edn, p. 209).

The *Perambulation* was intended to be the first of a series of county descriptions by Lambarde; but as he pointed out (pp. 474–5) – '*Britannia*, wherein . . . he hath not only farre exceeded whatsoever hath been attempted in that kynd, but hath also passed the expectation of other men and even his [Camden's] hope' – the *Britannia* forestalled Lambarde's larger intention and was better than he could hope to achieve. Yet this praise of Camden's work is somewhat offset by Lambarde's suggestion that the historical topography of a county could best be studied by one who dwelt within its borders. 'Nevertheless,' he says, 'being assured that the Inwardes of each place may best be knowen by such as reside therein, I can not but still encourage some one able man in each Shyre to undertake his owne [shire], whereby both many good particularities will come to discoverie every where, and Master Camden him selfe may yet have greater choice wherewith to amplifie and enlarge the whole.' Lambarde knew well the vivid 'particularities' in the disordered notes of Leland and perhaps unreasonably regretted their absence from the *Britannia*. He could hardly have foreseen that his wish for county volumes would be largely fulfilled in later decades, though not in time for Camden to use most of them.

Besides his indebtedness to the *Perambulation*, Camden had access to Lambarde's unpublished *Dictionarium Angliae Topographicum et Historicum*, which was not printed until 1730. It was a topographical dictionary with valuable guidance on place-names. That Lambarde was a good scholar of Old English is evident in the *Perambulation*; and his completion of the paraphrase of the Anglo-Saxon laws, begun by Laurence Nowell, reveals the depth of his knowledge of our early language.

Of a still earlier generation was John Twyne (d. 1581), who like Camden was a schoolmaster. Like Cotton later in the century, he collected

Roman coins and pottery and took an interest in megalithic monuments and in earthworks, all of which were to be found in the neighbourhood of Canterbury where he lived. Camden cites 'the learned John Twine' as an authority for the former existence of a land-bridge between England and the Continent (Gough edn, p. 220).

Richard Carew (d. 1620), whose *Survey of Cornwall* was published in 1602, was Camden's fellow undergraduate at Oxford and they had further opportunities for meeting during Carew's membership of Clement's Inn and of the Middle Temple over a period of about four years until 1577. There is a possibility that it was Camden who persuaded Carew in 1585 to revise his manuscript of the *Survey* and bring it up to date. In his opening address 'To the Reader', Carew says: 'When I first composed this treatise, not minding that it should be published in print, I caused only certain written copies to be given to some of my friends, and put Prosopopeia [an imaginary speaker] into the book's mouth. But since that time, Master Camden's often mentioning this work, and my friends' persuasions have caused my determination to alter, and to embrace a pleasing hope that charity and good construction [favourable interpretation] resteth now generally in all readers', etc. Camden referred to this forthcoming work in the earlier editions of the *Britannia*; in the fifth edition of 1594 he says that he cannot withhold the acknowledgement of his own indebtedness to Carew's work. In the 1607 edition (Gough edn, p. 6), having referred to Edgecombe, he continues: 'Near this is *Anthony*, remarkable for its neatness and for a pool ..., but much more remarkable for it[s] lord, Richard *Carew*, who not only maintains the dignity of this family, but reflects additional lustre to it by his virtues.' Carew returned the compliment, referring to Camden eight times in the body of the *Survey*. On Carew's death in 1620 his old friend wrote his epitaph (edn of 1969, p. 318) and made three errors of fact in a total of sixty-eight words. The inscription actually placed near Carew's grave was by another hand.

The topographic arrangement of the *Survey of Cornwall* is by hundredal divisions; Lambarde's *Perambulation of Kent* winds about that county with some measure oi continuity: neighbouring places are described in sequence with few breaks. The *Britannia* follows the coasts and the major rivers, filling in between them in a fairly orderly fashion, but missing not a few things on the way for no apparent reason other than the necessity for brevity in a work covering the whole of Britain as opposed to the description of one shire. In Sussex, for instance, he omits Halnaker, Parham and Danny Park, all great houses; Boxgrove Priory, Bayham Abbey and Horsham town; in Surrey he ignores Newark Priory and Haslemere town; and in Kent, the castles of Hever, Sissinghurst and Scotney, houses such as Knole and Ightham Mote, as well as West Malling Abbey. The lists for each of these counties could be further extended to include places significant in Camden's day and comparable with places that he does mention.

Another antiquary to whom he acknowledges his indebtedness was Thomas Talbot, clerk of the records in the Tower and compiler of manuscript collections, some of which found their way into the Cottonian library. 'In the succession of earls,' says Camden, 'not to conceal my obligations to any, I must acknowledge myself under very great ones to Thomas Talbot, a diligent examiner of records, and perfect master of our antiquities' (Gough edn, p. cxlviii).

Among the many who corresponded with Camden and provided him with information was George Owen (d. 1613), who in 1603 published his *Description of Pembrokeshire*; and another was Sampson Erdeswicke (d. 1613) whose *Survey of Staffordshire* was completed in the year of his death. But he was more interested in the county families and their residences than in general topography. A third local antiquary, Mr St Loe Kniveton of Derbyshire, was left £3 by Camden, who expressly recorded his gratitude to him for material used in the Derbyshire chapter of the *Britannia* (Gough edn, II, p. 301).

John Selden (d. 1654), the jurist and antiquary of the Middle Temple; Sir Henry Savile (d. 1622), translator of Tacitus' *Histories*, and his brother Thomas (d. 1593), an antiquary who corresponded with Camden; Sir Henry Spelman (d. 1641), student of Old English and church historian; Sir Henry Wotton (d. 1639), the scholarly ambassador; Sir Edward Hobey (d. 1617), 'my particular friend' (Gough edn, p. 214), translator from French and Spanish, who became a favourite of James I – these and other distinguished men were content to regard the old schoolmaster as a familiar acquaintance.

Closest of all to him was Cotton; but John Stow the tailor (d. 1605), antiquary and collector of chronicles, 'the most accurate and businesslike of the historians of the century' (*D.N.B.*), must also have spent much time in Camden's company. Like Cotton, Stow had collected a library and made its contents available to his friends – and this in spite of poverty. In his chapter on the Danes (Gough edn, p. cxx), Camden cites the work of 'Dudo de St. Quintin a very antient author in the library of John Stowe, the industrious London antiquary, to which I have always free access'. There Camden was able to make use of a transcript of Leland's *Itinerary* and of a large collection of other important topographical works.

Yet even more valuable was the library of Archbishop Parker (d. 1575), one of Camden's early patrons. In it were to be had many precious Old English manuscripts rescued from destruction at the dissolution of the monasteries; and not a few of these texts were otherwise unknown. It formed a complement to Cotton's library, which was collected later, after the greater part of the Parker collection had passed to Corpus Christi College, Cambridge. Parker was also responsible, mainly through his amanuenses, for the earliest editions of several Saxon and medieval texts important to Camden in his work preparatory to the *Britannia*; and Parker's Latin secretary, John Joscelin (d. 1603), was an Anglo-Saxon scholar perhaps second only to Laurence Nowell (d. 1576), whose work was also to be of much benefit

to the Elizabethan antiquaries. Stow was another of those who was employed by Parker as an editor.

John Selden of the Inner Temple was one of the London antiquaries who possessed a library of more than ordinary antiquarian interest. The studies underlying his *Analecton Anglo-Britannicon* [British and English Literary Gleanings] of 1606, a chronological collection of records down to 1066, were probably available to Camden, at least in discussion, during the years preceding his edition of 1607. The antiquary Francis Tate (d. 1616), also of the Inner Temple, collected manuscripts in a more limited way. We know from Camden himself that the important document known as the *Tribal Hidage*, the original of which was probably compiled in the seventh century, was given to him by Tate (Gough edn, p. cxxx). It had once belonged to William Fleetwood and at some time had been copied by Lambarde.

Lord Lumley (d. 1609), a member of the Society of Antiquaries, had a considerable library, including a number of manuscripts from the monasteries. Some of these, especially those of antiquarian interest, were eventually acquired by Cotton. And Lord William Howard (d. 1640), although a baron of the Scottish border, formed a library composed mainly of works of history and heraldry. He was a friend of Cotton and Camden and in 1592 published an edition of the chronicle of Florence of Worcester which was of more than ordinary importance to the student of early medieval history. Camden called him 'an attentive and learned searcher into venerable antiquity'.

Besides the informal and intimate conversations that Camden could enjoy in the company of these many scholarly acquaintances, he took part in the more formal meetings of the Society of Antiquaries, of which many of his friends were members. Besides Cotton, at whose house they met, and Francis Tate, the secretary, there were Stow, the Spelmans (Sir Henry and Sir John), Lord Lumley, the heralds William Dethick and

Francis Thynne, lawyers such as Sir John Dodderidge, the Solicitor-General, and William Fleetwood, the Recorder of London, George Hakewill (d. 1649), the Archdeacon of Surrey and Arthur Agarde (d. 1615), an exchequer official who presented papers to the Society on such topics as the antiquity of the shires, of Parliament and of the Inns of Court. He also did something to elucidate the Domesday Book. Occasional visitors included Lambarde, Carew and Erdeswicke. In his revisions for the later editions of the *Britannia* Camden must have benefited much from the learned discussions that occupied the meetings of the Society. At the end of his life he was shown honour by some of the highest in the land, for his funeral procession included such old friends as Cotton and the members of the College of Arms, as well as some of the greater prelates and nobles.

Through his many friends and acquaintances the total range of manuscripts and printed books to which Camden had access is very remarkable and amply made up for the lack of a national collection. The library accumulated by Parker down to the time of his death and that amassed later by Cotton, together concentrated in and near London a wealth of material within easy reach. Parker's collection was at Lambeth, where Archbishop Bancroft began to form a permanent library in 1610; Cotton's was at his house in Westminster. Stow's library, too, was near by and there were smaller collections at the Middle Temple, as well as the greater libraries of the Inns of Court. Moreover, the muniments at the Guildhall have a bearing on the history of England as well as of London.

The magnitude of Camden's task can best be appreciated by a rather more detailed consideration of the range of sources available to a London antiquary in the late sixteenth century, making some realization possible of how vast were the studies preliminary to the writing of the *Britannia*. Of course, some of Camden's other works – those projected as well as those completed – made a contribution to the introductory chapters and to local detail in the main body of the work, especially where, as often happens, he relates local events to national history. His own edition of the chronicles of Thomas of Walsingham, of William of Jumièges, with part of that of Geoffrey Baker (though then wrongly attributed to Sir Thomas de la More), Asser's *Life of Alfred* and the Giraldus Cambrensis, all published in one book in 1603 at Frankfurt, gave him an intimate knowledge of these texts.

As mentioned in the preface Professor Douglas has said that the 'Britannia is essentially Roman Britain as seen in relation to its later growth'; and indeed the whole plan of the work is determined by the tribal organization in being at the time of the Claudian conquest. Classical texts were therefore crucial to Camden, and not merely those that were familiar to him as a schoolmaster. Caesar's *Commentaries* he knew well, but the printed editions of 1585 and later provided a convenient new text. There had been continental editions of Tacitus in the earlier part of the sixteenth century; later there was sufficient popular interest in his works in England for translations of the *Histories* and *Agricola* to appear in 1581, and the *Annals* and *Germania* in 1598, though, of course, Camden himself had no need of them in English. Printed editions of the elder Pliny's *Natural History* had been published on the Continent at varying intervals from 1473 onwards and Philemon Holland, translator in 1610 of the *Britannia*, produced an English rendering of Pliny in 1601. Diodorus Siculus, mentioned by Camden perhaps more often than his relevance justified, had appeared in print at Basel in 1548 and Strabo's *Geography* was presented in the original Greek four years earlier. Erasmus himself produced an edition of Ptolemy's *Geography* in 1533 and there were several other editions preceding that by Mercator in 1578. The *Antonine Itinerary*, a work fundamental to Camden's method, had been twice published abroad in the early sixteenth century; in England, Robert Talbot's manuscript notes on the British section is known to have been available to Leland, Lambarde and Camden. As Sir Thomas Kendrick has pointed out (*British Antiquity*, p. 135), this work afforded scholars what was essentially a skeletal map of Roman Britain. Also available, though less valuable for Camden's purpose, was the Peutinger Table, which had been discovered in 1507. Camden had learned of its details long before its publication. And the last of the essential classical sources that he used was the *Notitia Dignitatum*, printed at Basel in 1552. He refers to later works such as the *Panegyrici Latini*, the largely fictional *Historia Augusta*, *Ammianus Marcellinus* and the *Historia* of Orosius, but they are of no great consequence as his sources and all but the *Panegyrici* were available to him in sixteenth-century printed editions or in manuscripts. He could, however, have taken what he wanted of them from secondary sources.

The raw material for writing the history of fifth-century Britain was to hand in Polydore Vergil's edition of Gildas's *de Excidio* of 1525 and there was a manuscript copy of Nennius' *Historia Brittonum* in Cotton's library in 1617 which may well have been there a decade earlier. Cotton also possessed a number of the works fundamental to a reconstruction of the history of the Anglo-Saxons, including seven of the principal recensions of the Old English Chronicle, namely the manuscripts now usually known as Ā, A, B, C, D, E and F, the last of which is in English and Latin. This bilingual text had formerly been in Camden's own possession and the manuscript included Robert de Monte's Chronicle. The manuscript closest to the archetype of the Old English Chronicle, manuscript Ā, had been one of Archbishop Parker's treasured possessions and on his death in 1575 it passed, with much else from his library, to Corpus Christi College, Cambridge, in a binding that included texts of the laws of kings Ine and Alfred of Wessex, a list of popes and of archbishops to whom they had sent the pallium, as well as lists of English bishops and archbishops. Cotton also had one of the versions of the genealogy of the West Saxon kings down to Edward the Martyr (d. 978). Equally important for the Anglo-Saxon period was Bede's *Ecclesias-*

tical History. Cotton had two of the earliest and least corrupt texts and besides these Camden probably had access to one or more of the ten or so editions of Bede printed on the Continent. They range in date from 1475 to 1601. The version printed at Antwerp in 1550 was especially valuable in that it was a critical revision of the text based on good manuscripts.

Copies of the laws of the kings of Kent and Wessex were at one time or another in the possession of men known to Camden, some of them well known to him. Apart from Archbishop Parker and his Latin secretary John Joscelin (d. 1603), Selden had owned several of these texts. Some of the Parker copies of the laws are known to have been studied by Talbot, Nowell and Lambarde, as well as by Joscelin; and the *Textus Roffensis*, used by Parker and Lambarde, and probably known to Camden, comprised laws of the early Kentish kings, the laws of Alfred and the later West Saxon kings, genealogies of the Saxon and Anglian royal houses, lists of popes and emperors and of English bishops and archbishops, most of which were useful at least for preserving a relative chronology. There are also in the *Textus* binding the laws of the Conqueror and the *Institutiones henrici regis* (i.e. Henry I), besides a cartulary of the priory of Rochester Cathedral.

Other basic texts which Camden knew at first hand or in transcripts were the *Burghal Hidage*, bound in with manuscript A of the *Anglo-Saxon Chronicle*, which was in Cotton's library; and a manuscript of the *Tribal Hidage* which had belonged to William Fleetwood. Yet another Cottonian text that Camden refers to is that which recounts the revival of monasticism in tenth-century England; but the ownership of the manuscript of King Alfred's will, referred to several times in the *Britannia*, cannot be traced back before the early eighteenth century. Obviously, however, he had access to an original or a transcript of it, probably through the good offices of one of the London antiquaries.

Lastly among important documents of the Anglo-Saxon period, mention should be made of the land charters, which throw some light on several aspects of Anglo-Saxon history. It is doubtful, however, whether much of the indirect evidence that they afford to modern scholars was derivable from them by Camden and his contemporaries, however learned. Certainly there is little in the *Britannia* to suggest it. Yet scores of charters were to be found in Cotton's library (Sawyer, *Anglo-Saxon Charters*, pp. 50–54) and Parker had possessed many too (ibid., pp. 44–5). There were others at the College of Arms, at Lambeth Palace, at the Guildhall (ibid., pp. 57–8), St Paul's (ibid., p. 61), Westminster Abbey (ibid., p. 62), and above all in the royal records, of which Domesday Book was an important item. This latter source was not printed until 1783, but the original was easily accessible to Camden and he cites it from time to time, especially in his remarks on the earlier history of the towns.

About two hundred manuscripts of Geoffrey of Monmouth's *History of the Kings of Britain* are known to exist and some no doubt have been lost. Printed editions appeared in Paris in 1508 and 1517 and in Heidelberg in 1587. A text of one kind or another was to be had in Elizabethan London, for Camden and his contemporaries obviously used one; but he, unlike Leland, largely rejected it and it is of little significance in relation to the *Britannia*.

Of the other numerous medieval sources only a few of the main ones need to be noticed here. As was said earlier, Camden himself had edited Asser's *Life of Alfred*, the chronicles of Walsingham and Jumièges and some of the works of Baker and Cambrensis. It was natural that he should cite these most familiar works rather more often than their relevance warranted. The works of William of Malmesbury, or at least some of them, could be consulted in Lord Lumley's library and Matthew Paris was readily accessible in Stow's edition of 1571. Stow's other editions, such as his Matthew of Westminster of 1567 and his *Chronicles of England* of 1580 were also easily available. Henry of Huntingdon's *History of the English* came later, in 1597, among Savile's *Rerum Angli-*

carum Scriptores post Bedam, but in good time for the expanded editions of the *Britannia*. Higden's *Polychronicon* was to be had in a transcript by Nowell as well as in Caxton's edition of 1480. The fact that William Howard was able to translate Florence of Worcester's *Chronicon ex Chronicis* in 1592 makes it likely that a manuscript was available to the London antiquaries, of which Howard was one. Similarly, Camden's use of one of Walter Map's works, those of John of Salisbury and of others, was made possible either by the accessibility of the original manuscripts or by transcripts of them.

The number of printed works on topographical subjects was few and apart from Lambarde's *Perambulation of Kent*, which Camden acknowledged that he used extensively, of no great help; but there was Leland's unpublished and invaluable *Itinerary* to be drawn on copiously, probably in John Stow's transcript of it. The extent of Camden's debt to Leland was amply demonstrated by Gough in his 'Additions' to the edition of 1789, in which he cites the *Itinerary* often at considerable length. This has been done also in the present edition not simply to reveal the sometimes frequent dependence of the one topographer upon the other, but because of the intrinsic interest of Leland's observations and their illumination of Camden's text.

Leland's was an unfinished work that would probably have remained unfinished even had he retained his sanity and lived long enough to have been able to complete it. Its merit, even where it consists only of rough jottings, is the immediacy of his descriptions: the notes seem often to have been made on the spot as he stood, or sat his horse, viewing a building. Camden, on the other hand, generalizes and seldom gives the reader an impression of first-hand witness. One of the very few instances of his deliberate showing of first-hand knowledge occurs in his paragraph on Wallingford (Gough edn, p. 148). Speaking of the castle, he confesses: 'Its size and magnificence used to strike me with astonishment when I came thither a lad from Oxford, it being a retreat for the students of Christ Church.' But there was little room in the *Britannia* for such things. In order to keep it within manageable compass, he was forced to eschew detail and to compress his descriptions, so much so that many of them are lacking in the kind of particularity that serves to make memorable distinctions. Occasionally, his reference to places is so perfunctory as to be hardly worth the space they occupy in the text.

But the point in which he differs most essentially from Leland is in his constantly associating places with people, whereas Leland is interested in a place for its own sake, rather than for its antiquarian or human associations. He was primarily interested in the England of his own day; Camden was mainly concerned with the contemporary appearance of things only in so far as they illustrated the past, and preferably the distant past. As Kendrick so rightly says (*British Antiquity*, p. 150): 'There is no sense of joyous exploration in Camden's work. . . . In his slow-moving dignified description of Britain he found little room to record the erratic enthusiasms of his famous predecessor.' Nevertheless, he showed 'how great was the unexplored wealth of valid antiquarian evidence to be found by going to look for it'; and in this he set an example of research in the field – or rather along the highways and byways – that even today continues to influence topographical studies. And a further debt was owed to Leland, whose journeys between 1534 and 1543 had as their ostensible purpose the search for manuscripts to be included in Henry VIII's library, and although topography soon came to dominate his mind, he was not altogether unmindful of the King's commission to him. His *Itinerary* and even more the *Collectanea* contain numerous extracts from medieval chronicles that provided Camden with source material not otherwise available to

him, though he does not acknowledge his intermediate source. But he does cite and acknowledge Leland's poem *Cygnea Cantio* of 1545 (Gough edn, p. 211, and see also p. 117); and his *Assertio . . . Arthurii* of the previous year is the origin of some other of Camden's statements. This work of Leland's was intended as a counterblast to Polydore Vergil's assertions that Geoffrey of Monmouth had mingled fact with fiction in his *History* and particularly in his account of King Arthur. Leland admitted that Geoffrey made some mistakes, but sought to rebut the charge that parts of the work were fictional. Leland's fanatical patriotism stifled any critical sense he might have brought to bear on Geoffrey's work; yet already in the first edition of the *Britannia* in 1586, Camden leaned towards Polydore Vergil's view.

But Camden himself was certainly not scrupulous in his use of evidence. In the notes to the present edition a number of instances will be found where he has altered an early form of a place-name in order that it should the better fit into some preconceived notion that he had of its origin. Professor Douglas (*English Scholars*, p. 23) says of seventeenth-century scholars that 'sometimes they allowed the intensity of their beliefs to distort their use of evidence' and (ibid., p. 165): 'Neither Commelin nor Camden displayed a sufficient regard for accuracy or a nice discrimination in their choice of materials.' Yet with all his faults, in genealogy, in the handling of evidence and, if indeed it can be called a fault, in his omissions of significant places comparable with those he includes, Camden's achievement in the *Britannia* remains among the greatest in sixteenth-century scholarship. His work is of enduring value to all who seek to explain the detailed features of the face of Britain.

ABBREVIATIONS USED IN THE NOTES

Additions	Gough's Additions to his translation of 1789
Arch. Journ.	Archaeological Journal
Arch. Sussex	The Archaeology of Sussex
A.S. Charters	Anglo-Saxon Charters
A.S. Chron.	The Anglo-Saxon Chronicle
Bede (E.H. or H.E.)	Ecclesiastical History of the English People (Plummer)
B. of E.	The Buildings of England series
Brit.	Britannia, a History of Roman Britain
Camb. Hist. Eng. Lit.	Cambridge History of English Literature
Coastline	The Coastline of England and Wales
Dic.	The Concise Oxford Dictionary of English Place-Names
D.N.B.	Dictionary of National Biography
Domesday Geog. S.E. Eng.	The Domesday Geography of South-East England
E.H.D.	English Historical Documents
Elements	English Place-Name Elements
Eng. River N.	English River-Names
E.P.D.	English Pronouncing Dictionary
E.P.N.S.	English Place-Name Society
Etym. Dic.	The Oxford Dictionary of English Etymology
Hist. Geog. Eng.	An Historical Geography of England before A.D. 1800
Lamb.	A Perambulation of Kent (Lambarde)
Lang. & Hist.	Language and History in Early Britain
Lost Villages	The Lost Villages of England
L.T.S.	Itinerary in England and Wales in or about the Years 1535–1543
Med. Arch.	Medieval Archaeology
Med. Eng.	Medieval England: an aerial survey
New Towns	New Towns of the Middle Ages: Town Plantations in England, Wales and Gascony
Norman Conquest	The Norman Conquest: its Setting and Impact
The Normans	The Normans and the Norman Conquest
Orig. E.P.N.	The Origin of English Place-Names
Oxf. Hist.	Oxford History of England
P.N. Surrey	The Place-Names of Surrey
P.N. Sussex	The Place-Names of Sussex
Public Records	An Introduction to the Use of the Public Records
S.E. Eng.	An Archaeology of South-East England
Surnames	The Penguin Dictionary of Surnames
Surrey Arch. Coll.	Surrey Archaeological Collections
Sussex Arch. Coll.	Sussex Archaeological Collections
Two Saxon Chrons.	Two of the Saxon Chronicles Parallel
V.C.H.	Victoria County Histories

REGNI · SURREY AND SUSSEX

SELECT BIBLIOGRAPHY

References to the companion volume on Kent
are given as *Kent*

Archaeological Journal, CII, 1945; CV, Supplement, 1950;
CXXVII, 1970

Archaeology of Surrey, The, D. C. Whimster, 1931

Buildings of England, The: Surrey, I. Nairn and N.
Pevsner, 1962

Domesday Geography of South-East England, The, H. C.
Darby and E. M. J. Campbell (eds.), 1962, 364f.

Little Guides, The: Surrey, J. C. Cox and P. M. John-
ston, 5th edn, 1926

List of Antiquities . . . in Surrey, C. D. Hawley (ed.), 4th
edn, 1951

Place-Names of Surrey, The, J. E. B. Gover, A. Mawer
and F. M. Stenton with collaboration of A. Bonner,
1934

Surrey Archaeological Collections, XXI, 1908; XXXIX,
1931; XL, 1932; LI, 1940; LVIII, 1961

Victoria County History, The: Surrey, 4 vols., 1902–12

The General Bibliography is on page 75

REGNI

NEXT to the Attrebatii on the east were the REGNI,[01] or, as Ptolomy[02] calls them *PHΓNOI*,[a] inhabiting the parts now commonly called Surrey and Southsex, with the sea coast of Hants. I purposely omit what has occurred to me as the etymology of the name, as perhaps not well founded, if I should suppose Ptolomy called them *Ρηγνοι* because they formed a *kingdom*,[b] and were allowed by the Romans to preserve a regal form of goverment. For in this tract Cogidunus[04] the British king had, according to Tacitus,[05] some cities given him agreeable to the antient practice of the Roman people, that they might have even kings for the instruments of their bondage.[c] But as this conjecture neither appears probable to myself, nor is likely to be approved by others, I entirely reject it, and readily embrace the Saxon origin of the modern names which is founded in truth; *Southsex* from the South Saxons, and *Suthrey* from their southern situation on the river;[06] for that this is the meaning of *Suth-rey* none can deny who considers that *Over-rhey* signifies in old English *on the other side of the River*.[07]

a. Some MSS. of Ptolemy have *ΡηγΙνοι* [*sic*], and so Selden. Gale's MS. n. [03]

b. *Regnum.*

c. for their slaves G. [See n. 03.]

01 The *Regni*, more correctly the *Regnenses*, seem to take their name from the kingdom (*regnum*) of King (*rex*) *Cogidubnus*. Their territory included parts of Surrey, East Sussex and most of West Sussex. See *Town and Country in Roman Britain*, pp. 158-9.

02 Claudius Ptolemaeus of C2 was an Egyptian geographer, astronomer and mathematician. His *Geography* takes in the whole of the world then known. See fig. I, 'The British Isles according to Ptolemy', in O.S. *Map of Roman Britain*, text p. 20.

03 On Selden see p. 26, n. 07. Thomas Gale (1635?-1702), Dean of York, produced a series of volumes in Latin which were editions of chronicles and early historians. His younger son Samuel Gale (1682-1754) annotated a copy of Gibson's edition of Camden's *Britannia*, which Gough acquired. He added Samuel's annotations as footnotes to the edition of 1789, distinguishing them as *MS. n. Gale*.

04 Tacitus in the *Agricola*, 14 (H. Mattingly's trans., p. 64), says that: 'Certain states were presented to King Cogidubnus, who maintained his unswerving loyalty down to our own times – an example of the long-established Roman custom of employing even kings to make others slaves.' An inscription found in Chichester (*Noviomagus Regnensium*) in 1723 records that 'By the authority of Tiberius Claudius Cogidubnus, king and legate of the Emperor in Britain, this temple is dedicated to Neptune and Minerva &c.' See *Arch. Journ.* XCII, 396-7. The large and luxurious villa discovered at Fishbourne, close to Chichester, 'is of palatial scale...which might well accord with the senatorial status of the royal house of Cogidubnus, though the building seems a little late for the King-Legate' (*Archaeology of Roman Britain*). Cornelius Tacitus (b. circa A.D. 55) held high office in Rome and the provinces. In 77 he married the daughter of Agricola whose biography he wrote in 98. This work is significant in the history of Britain in that Agricola had been its governor. The *Germania*, also of A.D. 98, is a study of the German tribes including those which were ancestral to the Angles, Saxons and Jutes. His later works, the *Histories* and the *Annals*, have less relevance to Britain. The *Agricola* and *Germania* have appeared as a Penguin Classic (*On Britain and Germany*). See also p. 16, n. 40, *Kent*.

05 See previous note and reference there.

06 See n. 08 below.

07 See n. 08 below.

THIS county, called by Bede *Suthriona*,[a] commonly *Suth-rey* and *Surrey*, by the Saxons from its south situation on the river 'Suth-rea', ('Suth', signifying in their language *South* and 'rea' *a river*),[08] is bounded on the west by Berks and Hants; on the south by Sussex; on the east it borders on Kent; and is divided from Middlesex to the north by the Thames. It is of no great extent, but very rich, and in the level parts near the Thames produces some corn, but mostly grass, especially to the south, where runs a continued deep valley, antiently called from the woods *Holmesdale*,[09] and affording an agreeable prospect diversified with woods, corn-fields and meadows. From hence succeed a long ridge of hills,[10] parks well stocked with deer, and rivers with fish, affording plenty of game both for hunting and fishing. Some have compared it to a garment, whose contexture is both fine and coarse, with a green fringe, its inner parts being barren, but its outer or hem fertile. In surveying this county I shall follow the course of the Thames and other rivers, by which means I shall leave no remarkable places unnoticed, all places of considerable antiquity lying on these rivers.

To go down the Thames; this river after leaving Berks washes *Chertsey*,[b] which Bede calls *Cerotus'*[11] isle,[c] now scarce a peninsula except in winter floods; in which, as in a spot unfrequented by men, Frithwald, who styles himself in his charter[12] of foundation, "petty prince of the province of the

a. Sudergeona, 'Suthrigena'. Eccl. Hist. IV. 6. [See n. 08.]
b. Sax. 'Ceortesige'. [See n. 11.]
c. Hist. Eccl. IV. 6. *Cerotaesei*, i.e. *Ceroti insula*. [See n. 11.]

08 In fact, Bede's original Latin text, according to the oldest surviving MSS, had *Sudergeona* (as in Gough's note a), in the genitive plural. The *Anglo-Saxon Chronicle* varies between *Suthrig(e)*, *Suth(e)rege*, in the nominative. The first element was Old English *sūther*, 'south, southern'; and the *Chronicle* forms have *gē*, 'region', as final element; but Bede used a related word meaning 'inhabitants of a region'. Both of these words became obsolete early in the Anglo-Saxon period. The total meaning '(inhabitants of) the southern region or district' makes sense only in relation to Middlesex, '(the land) of the Middle Saxons'. Camden's guess that the place-name Surrey signified 'south' in relation to the Thames rested on the false assumption that its second element was -*rea*. A river-name Rea occurs in Cambs., Salop, Worcs. and Warwicks., and is derived from the Old English phrase (*æt*) *thǣre ēa*, '(at) the water or river'. When earlier he says that *Over-rhey* signifies in Old English 'on the other side of the river' he was correct; Overy, Oxon.; (Burnham) Overy, Norfolk; and (St Mary) Overy, now Southwark Cathedral, are instances of this place-name usage; but he was wrong in identifying the -*rey* of Surrey with the final element of Overy. To support his etymology he cites a spelling -*rea* which probably never occurred; of the twenty-seven forms quoted in *P.N. Surrey*, p. 1, the nearest to it is *Southray* in a document of 1380. Ray, as it happens, is an alternative modern form of Rea; and there are rivers so named in Oxon. and Wilts.

09 The place-name 'Holmesdale' is probably a coinage of C16. 'Dale' is not found in older Surrey place-names, but Old English *denu* (usually now -dean, -den(e)) instead. It has the same meaning as 'dale' and occurs at least thirty-six times in the county. 'Holmes-' in this place-name is presumably from OE *holegn*, 'holly', a tree still common in the woods there. With the North Downs scarp-face defining the one side and an irregular sandstone ridge intermittently marking the other, this is still one of the most beautiful of southern English valleys at any time of the year. See also p. 11, n. 66.

10 The term 'Northdownes' was already in use c. 1570 (*P.N. Surrey*, p. 8) so that it is somewhat strange that Camden did not use it.

11 *Cerotus* was a British personal name, one of relatively few surviving in English place-names. See my *English Place-Names & Their Origins*, p. 136. The second element of Chertsey was Old English *ēg*, 'island, well-watered land'.

12 Camden could not have known that this charter may be spurious,

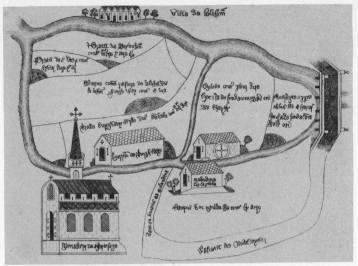

Chertsey Abbey, a plan of the demesne from the Exchequer Ledger

Surreians under Wulpher[13] king of the Mercians," and Erchenwald[14] bishop of London, in the early ages of the English church, founded a small monastery, which was some considerable time the burying place of the devout king Henry VI.[15] whom the house of York dethroned and took off to secure the crown to themselves, and interred here without any honour. He was afterwards removed to Windsor, and received all funeral honours from Henry VIII. who deposited him in his new chapel,[16] and was such an admirer of his holy virtues, a pattern of Christian piety and patience, that he applied to Pope Julius[17] to rank him among the Saints.* But the Pope's avarice prevented this, demanding so exhorbitant a sum of money for his cannonization that he seemed to have more regard to money than the king's sanctity. Below this the little river *Wey*, which rises in Hampshire, falls into the Thames, and at its entrance into Surrey visits *Feornham*, now *Farnham*, called from the fern growing about it,[18] which Ethelbald[19] king of the West Saxons gave to "the bishop and congregation of the church of Winton."[20] Here about 893 king Alfred with a small force routed the ravaging Danes;[21] and afterwards when king

*Hist. Cantuar. [History of Canterbury?]

although it does contain some genuine elements. In it, some time during the years between 666 and 674, *Wulfhere* confirmed a grant of land by *Frithuwald*, sub-king (*subregulus*), to *Eorcenwald* and Chertsey Abbey. See *A.S. Charters*, p. 89 and cp. *Oxf. Hist.* II, 54–5.

There is a translation of this charter in *E.H.D.* I, 440–41. Only a few fragments of the great abbey are still visible. See *B. of E. Surrey*, pp. 129–30.

13 *Wulfhere* (d. 674) was son of the powerful heathen king *Penda*, and was the first Mercian king to be baptized.

14 *Eorcenwald* (d. 693) became bishop of the East Saxons with his see in London, in 676. He founded Barking Abbey also. Bede, *E.H.* IV, 6.

15 Henry VI was murdered in 1471 and his remains were re-interred in St George's Chapel, Windsor, in 1484, where his monument is now a black slab with his funeral helmet above.

16 It was hardly 'his new chapel', for only the chancel vault was built in his reign and even this had been contracted for three years before his accession in 1509. *B. of E. Berks*, p. 268.

17 Julius II, pope from 1503 to 1513.

18 The meaning of this place-name is 'enclosure or enclosed place (*hamm*) amongst the fern or bracken'. *P.N. Surrey*, p. 169.

19 Æthelbald ruled Wessex from 856 to 860 after supplanting his father Æthelwulf. On the latter's death, Æthelbald married his own step-mother, Judith, who was the daughter of Charles the Bald, King of the West Franks. His youngest brother became King Alfred the Great. See *Oxf. Hist.* II, 231, n. 1, and p. 243.

20 In fact, this doubtful charter records a grant by St Swithun, Bishop of Winchester, in 858 to Æthelbald of land at Farnham on lease for the king's lifetime, with a reversion to the Cathedral of Winchester. *A.S. Charters*, p. 370, no. 1274.

21 The Danish defeat at Farnham in 893 was at the hands of Edward, son of Alfred. See *Oxf. Hist.* II, 263, for details.

22 Henry de Blois (d. 1171) was the younger brother of King Stephen. As abbot of Glastonbury and bishop of Winchester, he had the wealth to become a great builder of castles as well as ecclesiastical buildings. He became papal legate in 1139, but failed in his ambition to become archbishop of Canterbury. An unscrupulous politician during the anarchy of Stephen's reign, he changed sides to suit his own purposes. William of Malmesbury calls him 'an unheard of monstrosity'.

23 Henry of Blois probably built the square tower, surrounded by a mound at its base, discovered in the excavations of 1958. (*Med. Arch.* IV, 1960, 81f.) It was begun in the same year, 1138, as were his castles at Taunton (Som.), Downton (Wilts.), Merdon and Bishops Waltham (Hants.) and the keep at Wolvesey (Winchester). The surviving shell-keep at Farnham was probably built in later C12 to replace the tower demolished by Henry II in 1155. The hill referred to by Camden is the natural one on which the whole complex of the castle buildings stands and not the mound within the shell-keep. For the whole matter see *B. of E. Surrey*, pp. 198–202. Today Farnham is one of the least spoiled towns of southern England and the view along Castle Street is as pleasing a townscape as any in Britain.

24 Probably Henry II; see previous note.

25 Waverley was the first Cistercian house in England. Only fragments of some of the buildings remain and they are visually unsatisfying in spite of the pleasing locality. Material removed from this abbey was used in the building of Loseley House (p. 5, n. 32) between 1561 and 1569. *B. of E. Surrey*, p. 302, n. There is a plan of the Abbey in *Abbeys*, H.M.S.O., 1959, fig. 14, 1.

Farnham Castle in 1761 after rebuilding, with the keep of the old castle in the background, engraved by Godfrey after Francis Grose

Stephen gave leave to all who followed his party to build castles, Henry Blois,[22] his brother and bishop of Winchester, erected one on a hill [23] that commands the town, which being a retreat for rebels was razed by Henry III.[24] but afterwards rebuilt by the bishops of Winchester, to whom it still belongs. At *Waverley* [25] William Gifford bishop of Winchester [26] founded [d] a small house for monks of the Cistercian order. From hence the Wye [27] runs through *Godelming*,[28] which king Alfred bequeathed to his brother's son Ethelwald,[29] not far from the manor of *Catteshull* [30] held by Hamo de Gatton "as

d. 1128. [See n. 25.]

26 Gifford (Giffard) held the see from 1100 to 1129 after being Chancellor to Rufus.

27 Wye is, of course, the Wey, the two names originally being identical. The derivation is uncertain though undoubtedly pre-English. See *Eng. River N.*, pp. 451–4 (Wey and Wye) and cp. *P.N. Glos.*, 1964, pp. 14–15 (Wye).

28 Godalming is an attractive country town in a friendly countryside.

29 Æthelwald was bequeathed the king's residence at Guildford also. For a translation of Alfred's Will see *E.H.D.* I, 492f., where it is dated between 873 and 888. The *Chronicle* annals for 901 and 904 speak of Æthelwald's rebellious actions and 905 records his death in battle in East Anglia. The correct dates are 899, 903 and 904 respectively. See p. 29, n. 11.

30 Catteshall, meaning 'hill frequented by wild cats' or 'hill of

4

Waverley Abbey in 1760, engraved by Godfrey
after Francis Grose

Mareshall of the women, when the king came thither;"[31] nor far from *Loseley*,[32] where I saw a beautiful house of the knightly family of More[33] in a park of oaks; and comes to *Guilford*,[34] Saxon 'Guld-ford',[35] and in some copies *Geglford*, now a considerable and handsome market town, with several inns; formerly a royal vill of the Saxon kings, bequeathed to Æthelwald aforesaid by his uncle.[36] Here is a palace[37] now going to decay, and not far from the river are the ruined walls of a large old castle.[38] In the middle of the town is the church,[39]

a man called Catt' (*P.N. Surrey*, p. 196), has a few fragments of what may have been a C13 chapel. 'Hamo de Gatton holds the manor of *Gateshull* in the county of Surrey from the lord King by serjeanty, which shall be the provision of twelve charwomen (*meretrices*) when the lord King shall come into these parts; and he shall not hold it except at the will of the King himself.' *Arch. Journ.* CV, 82 and note with reference.

31 This official was subordinate to the king's marshal and had delegated to him the duty of arranging

lodgings for the women servants of the court when it was on its peregrinations with the king from manor to manor. It was easier for the king to move round eating the produce of his lands than for it to be brought to him.

32 Loseley is 'the best house of its date in the county' (*B. of E. Surrey*, pp. 301–4 and pl. 21b). It was built 1561–9, but only the north wing remains.

33 Sir William More (1520–1600) built much of Loseley, using material from Waverley Abbey

(n. 25 above). His father, Sir Christopher More (d. 1549) was Sheriff of Surrey and Sussex. Sir George More (1553–1632) built Baynard's Park 'some time after 1587' (*B. of E. Surrey*, p. 89), but it has been much altered. The family monuments are to be seen in the Loseley Chapel at St Nicholas, Guildford. See *B. of E. Surrey*, p. 235, and *Surrey Arch. Coll.* XXXIX, 54–5.

34 Guildford is still 'a considerable and handsome market town' (Camden) with 'an almost perfect example of a bright and cheerful Home Counties [High] street' (*B. of E. Surrey*, p. 240). At least one of the inns known to Camden, The Angel, survives with a thirteenth-century crypt. Two other buildings in the High Street, Nos. 115 and 28, have cellars of the same date (*Arch. Journ.* CV, 82–4). There remain an unusually large number of fine older buildings in the town. For details see *B. of E. Surrey*, p. 229f.

35 The meaning was probably 'ford where golden flowers grew' (*P.N. Surrey*, pp. 9–10). Recently (*E.P.N.S. Journ.* II, 38) it has been suggested that the ford was at St Catherine's and that the name of the ford is characterized by the golden sand of the hill. *Geglford* is probably a scribal error.

36 See n. 29 above.

37 This may refer to 'The king's house ... granted by Charles to Murray earl of Anandale ... which was sold and pulled down 1630'. Gough, *Additions*, p. 173.

38 This was a royal stronghold and is now represented by a tower keep of c. 1170, with much Roman brick in its construction, set on an earlier motte. There are some fragments of subsidiary buildings and part of the outer gate in Castle Street is original also. *B. of E. Surrey*, pp. 235–6.

39 This is the fine church of St Mary's, Quarry Street. Its 'arched stone roof' is the vaulting of the chancel of c. 1220. The central tower is late Saxon. There are two other old churches in the town: St Nicholas, largely rebuilt in a shoddy manner in C19 (but see n. 33 above), and Holy Trinity, a 'handsome' building largely of 1749–63. *B. of E. Surrey*, pp. 231–5.

40 A *haga* originally meant 'hedge, enclosure' and in Late Old English 'a property'. Besides these 75 properties in Guildford, Domesday Book mentions another six. At a rough guess, the total population in 1086 was about 750. See *Domesday Geog. S.E. Eng.*, p. 398.

41 On Godwine see p. 31, n. 25; and see n. 43 below.

42 Æthelred II (978–1016) is usually referred to as the 'Unready', but more appropriately might have been called the 'Ineffective'. For his character see *Oxf. Hist.* II, 368–9.

43 The *Anglo-Saxon Chronicle*, MS 'C', under the year 1036, records these events thus:

In this year the innocent prince Alfred, son of King Æthelred came here [to England] and wished to go to his mother who was dwelling at Winchester; but earl Godwine would not allow him to [do so] and nor would other very powerful men because there was a strong sentiment favourable to Harold [Godwineson] although that was unjust.

But then Godwine prevented him, and
    placed him in captivity,
Dispersing his followers besides, slaying
    some in various ways;
Some of them were sold for money,
    some cruelly murdered,
Some of them were put in chains, and
    some of them were blinded,
Some were mutilated, and some were
    scalped.
No more horrible deed was done in this
    land
After the Danes came, and made peace
    with us here.
We can now but trust to the dear God
That they who without guilt were so
    pitiably killed
Rejoice joyfully in the presence of Christ.
Threatened with every kind of injury,
    the prince still lived
Until the decision was taken to convey
    him

Guildford, a mid-eighteenth-century view

whose east end with its arched stone roof seems of great antiquity. Here, as appears from William I's survey,[e] "the king had 75 *hagæ* or houses, in which dwelt 175 persons."[40] But nothing has rendered it so remarkable as the treachery and cruelty of Godwin earl of Kent,[41] who, A.D. 1036, when Alfred, son of king Ethelred[42] and heir to the crown of England, came from Normandy to claim his right, received him here with the most solemn assurances, which he soon broke. For falling suddenly in the night upon the 600 Normans who attended the royal youth, he decimated them, as our historians relate, and that not according to the antient manner, putting to death every tenth soldier by lot, but he put to death nine out of ten, and with excessive cruelty redecimated the remaining tenth men. As to Alfred, he delivered him up to Harold the Dane, who put out his eyes, and imprisoned him till his death.[43]

e. P. 30. [See n. 40.]

To the city of Ely, in chains as he was.
As soon as he arrived, his eyes were put
    out on board ship,
And thus sightless he was brought to the
    monks.
And there he remained as long as he
    lived.
Thereafter he was buried, as well
    became his rank,

With great ceremony, so honourable
    was he,
At the west end of the church, very near
    to the tower,
In the south aisle. His soul is with Christ.

(The translation of this verse is from Garmonsway, *A.S. Chronicle*, pp. 158, 160.)

6

The Wey, after a long course from hence north, in which it passes by no remarkable place except *Sutton*, the seat [44] of the knightly family of the *Westons*,[45] comes to *Woking* a royal mansion,[46] and *Pyriford*,[47] where in my time Edward, earl of Lincoln and baron *Clinton* built himself a house,[48] and near it *Ockeham*,[49] where the great philosopher William de Ockham, father of the sect of Nominal Philosophers,[50] received his birth and name. At the spot where it falls into the Thames by two channels, stands *Oatelands*,[51] a beautiful palace in a park, near

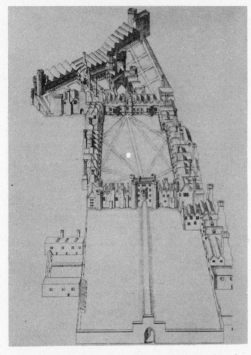

The Palace of Oatlands, from a drawing 'made about the time of Queen Elizabeth'

Material evidence for the massacre was very probably found on Guildown in 1929, partly overlying a cemetery of pagan Saxons of c6. Here were the skeletons of murdered men, the bodies having been tumbled some three or four at a time into shallow holes, hastily dug. Some had their arms behind their backs as though once bound there; some had been mutilated, with either arms, legs or heads severed

and the bones of these lying separate from the rest of the skeletons. For details see *Surrey Arch. Coll.* XXXIX, p. 1f., with photographs of the skeletons before they were disturbed by the excavators.

44 Sutton Place is 'the most important house of the years immediately after Hampton Court' (*B. of E. Surrey*, p. 398 and pl. 21a). It was probably built in the late

1520s and relatively new when Camden published the first edition of *Britannia* in 1586.

45 Sir Richard Weston (1466?–1542) was granted the manor in 1521. A later Sir Richard of the same family was the first to introduce the use of river-locks into England. *Surrey Arch. Coll.* LI, p. 101.

46 Remnants of this mansion survive as Woking Old Hall, the birthplace of Mary Tudor in 1514. See *B. of E. Surrey*, p. 336.

47 Pyrford, a shrunken village, retains some of its rural character with suburbia scarcely in sight. It is surprising that Camden makes no mention of Newark Priory, a foundation by Ruald de Calna (d. c. 1195) for Augustinian canons. Roofless and gaunt though the buildings are, they are lovely in their setting of willows and water-meadows beside the river Wey. For a plan and illustrations of the Priory and an account of its excavation see *Surrey Arch. Coll.* XL, 1f.

48 It was rebuilt by Sir John Wolley and this building in turn was demolished 'lately' by Lord Onslow (Gough, *Additions*, p. 173). Edward Fiennes de Clinton (1512–85) was created Earl of Lincoln in 1572. Among several high offices, he twice held that of Lord High Admiral. He was one of those who abandoned Lady Jane Grey in 1554.

49 Ockham may possibly be the birthplace of the Franciscan philosopher. He died at Munich c. 1349.

50 The nominalists maintained that genera and species are abstractions with no real existence except as words. Only the individual instance is real.

51 Oatlands, rebuilt from 1538 onwards, has only an archway and garden walls surviving above ground. Excavation of the site began in 1968. Materials from Abingdon Abbey were used in the building of this palace. *Med. Arch.* XII, 1968, 65.

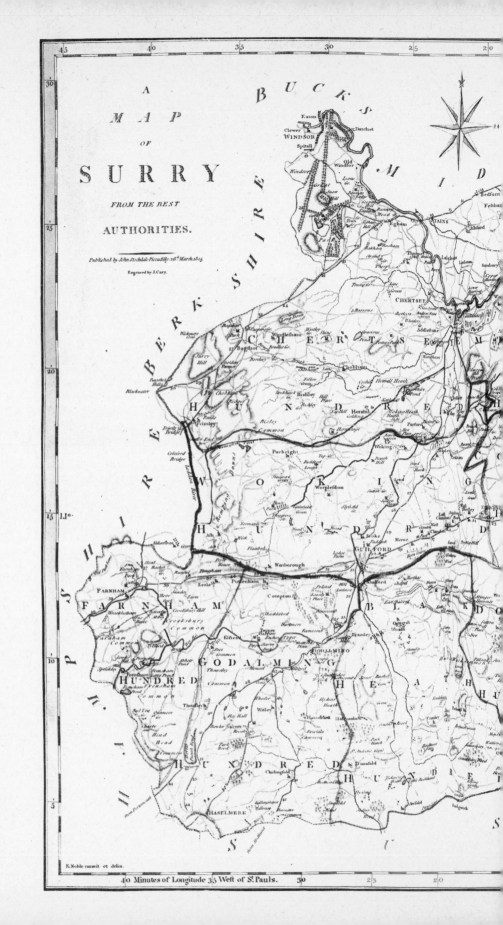

A
MAP
OF
SURRY
FROM THE BEST
AUTHORITIES.

Published by John Stockdale Piccadilly 26th March 1805

Engraved by J.Cary.

E. Noble curavit et delin.

40 Minutes of Longitude 35 West of St. Pauls. 30

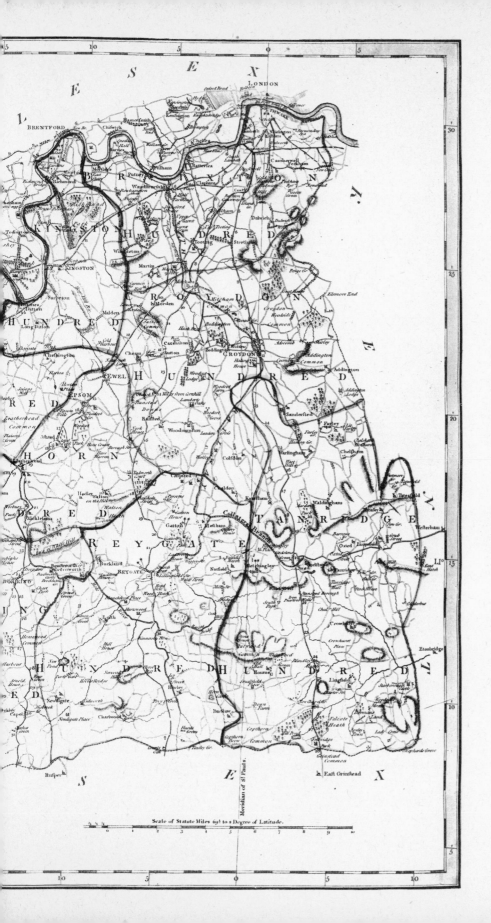

Scale of Statute Miles 69½ to a Degree of Latitude.

52 Bede's *E.H.* I, 2.

53 There is material evidence for a ford over the Thames at Oatlands in the discovery of a line of large flat stones across the bed of the river. The place-name Halliford ('holy ford') on the Middlesex side seems to confirm it (*Archaeology of Surrey*, p. 106). But Halliford may refer to a crossing of the little river Ash, rather than one over the Thames. In any case, many now consider that Caesar must have crossed the Thames at Brentford or London in 54 B.C. Sharpened stakes were found in the river at Brentford also; and there, or at the site of the future London, he was certainly nearer to the oppidum at Wheathampstead, Herts., of the Belgic chief Cassivel-launus (*Brit.*, p. 36). Moreover, stakes set in a river bed will usually be the remains of a fish weir.

54 A mistake for about 75 miles. Caesar, *Gallic War*, V, 2.

55 The Mole here passes through a gap in the North Downs.

56 The Mole partly disappears into 'swallows', fissures in the stream-bed, of which there are many between Boxlands and the Priory to the north, the greater number concentrated c. NG 165525. For the geological explanation see F. H. Edmunds, *The Wealden District*, 2nd edn, 1948, p. 72 and map p. 73. For old accounts of the 'swallows' see E. Parker, *Highways and Byways: East and Central Surrey*, 1937, p. 298; and Defoe, *A Tour..*, pp. 147–50, who presents the matter realistically. On a late C18 map of Surrey by Bowen the legend 'Here the River Mole runs under Ground', with a lengthy gap in the continuity of the stream, shows that like Camden he probably never visited the spot. Even in time of drought the stream runs without a break, though somewhat reduced in its flow.

57 The name of the Mole was formed from the place-name Molesey, *Mul's* island (*ēg*). Similar back-formations

which Cæsar crossed the Thames into Cassivelaun's territories: this being the only place where the Thames could be forded and that with great difficulty, which the Britans themselves in a manner discovered to Cæsar. On the other side this river was drawn up a large army of Britans, and the bank itself defended with sharp stakes driven into it, and some of the same were concealed under water in the bed of the river. "Remains of these, says Bede,[f] arc still to be seen, and it is evident, at first sight, that each of them is of the thickness of a man's thigh, covered with lead, and made fast in the bed of the river." But the Romans entered with so much intrepidity into the river up to their chins, that the Britans could not stand the shock, but abandoned the banks and fled. I cannot be mistaken in this, the river being scarce six feet deep hereabouts, and the place now called from these stakes *Coway stakes*.[53] Cassivelaun's territories are placed by Cæsar describing the passage at the distance of about 10 [54] miles from the sea which washes the east coast of Kent where he landed, and this ford of ours is at the same distance from the sea; of which passage I think I have now first revived the fleeting memorial.

A few miles east from hence the river *Mole* hastens to the Thames, having crossed the whole county from the south, and meeting with obstruction from some hills,[55] opens itself a subterraneous passage [56] like a *mole*, whence it seems to take its name,[57] as the famous river Anas (Guadiana) in Spain. There are no remarkable places on this river except at some distance from its rise, and near the old Roman military way called *Stanystreat*,[58] a town called *Aclea* or *Okeley*,[59] from the oaks

f. Ec. H. I. 2.[52]

of river-names are Wandle from Wandsworth; Arun from Arundel; and Chelmer from Chelmsford. *P.N. Surrey*, pp. 4–5.

58 Stane Street was constructed within a decade or so of the Roman Conquest in A.D. 43 to provide communication between Novio-magus (Chichester) and Londinium (London). Posting-stations on it are still traceable at Hardham, Sussex, and Alfoldean, Surrey, and the agger of the road itself remains visible in a few places along its course. For a detailed description see *Roman Ways in the Weald*, p. 45f., with strip maps.

59 Ockley was and is a village. The word 'town', from Old English *tūn*, underwent a development in meaning from 'enclosure', through 'farmstead', 'hamlet', 'village' until the Middle Ages, when it acquired its present sense. But even now, in some dialects, 'town' is used of something less than an urban complex of buildings. Perhaps, however, Camden was mistaken in his knowledge of the size of Ockley.

where Ethelwolph son of Egbert, who had taken holy orders,[60] from which he was by authority of the papal fee discharged, ascended his father's throne by hereditary right, and engaging the Danes, obtained the victory,[61] and slew the flower of their troops; but not much to the advantage of the kingdom, that Danish hydra always recovering itself. Not far from the head of this river is *Gatton*, now scarce a small village, though formerly a considerable town.[62] As a proof of its antiquity, Roman coins are found here,[63] and it sends two members to parliament. Lower lies *Rie-gate*, which, if derived from our antient language, signifies *the Course of the Stream*,[64] in the vale running far east, called *Holmesdale*,[65] whose inhabitants having once or twice routed the ravaging Danes make this rhyming boast:

> The Vale of Holmesdall
> Never wonne ne never shall.[66]

This town of Rhiegate is rather large than well built, having on the south a well wooded park in which Charles earl of Nottingham, baron *Effingham*,[67] and high admiral of England, has a house on the scite of a little monastery,[68] founded antiently by the earls of Warren and Surrey.[69] On the east side stood a castle, now neglected and decaying with age, built by the same earls, and commonly called *Holmes castle*[70] from the vale in

Today the Stane Street, noticeably raised on its Roman agger, runs beside the village green, around which are scattered a pleasing assortment of brick-and-tile village houses.

60 The story that Æthelwulf (839–55) had been 'educated by Swithhun for the Church, and ordained sub-deacon, but received a dispensation from Pope Leo IV because there was no other heir' is to be found in William of Malmesbury's *Gesta Pontificum Anglorum*, p. 160f. But 'the whole tale is a myth'. *Two Saxon Chrons.* II, 75.

61 It is most unlikely that Ockley was the scene of the battle between Æthelwulf and the Danes in 851 (correctly 850), though the *Anglo-Saxon Chronicle* implies that it took

place in Surrey. Early recorded forms of this place-name suggest that it meant '*Occa*'s wood' and this personal name probably recurs in Ockham (n. 49 above) and in Oxshott (Stoke D'Abernon parish). The *Chronicle* form is *Aclea*, 'oak wood'; but there is no surviving Surrey place-name that could reasonably be derived from this form. See *Oxf. Hist.* II, 242 and n. 3; *P.N. Surrey*, p. 276.

62 Gatton was probably never more than a village; today there is none. The records of an episcopal visitation of 1724–5 speak of two resident gentry and a population of 110 (*Surrey Arch. Coll.* XXXIX, 92). The church in medieval times could not have held many more. It was a rotten borough from the time it was

made a borough in 1450, when it began sending two members to Parliament, and in 1541, as the only inhabitant with voting rights, Sir Roger Copley returned both members by his one vote. It continued a rotten borough, with Reigate and Bletchingley, until the Reform Act of 1832.

63 Romano-British occupation is made the more certain by the discovery of Roman bricks here. *Archaeology of Surrey*, p. 148.

64 On Camden's misinterpretation of the first syllable of Reigate see p. 2, n. 08. This name is perhaps composed of Middle English *reye*, 'a roe-deer', and *gate*, a gap through which deer were driven in hunting. *P.N. Surrey*, pp. 304–5.

65 See p. 2, n. 09.

66 'Was never won [conquered] and never shall be.' *Lamb.*, pp. 468–9, suggested that this vaunt was the outcome of a Danish defeat in 904 and of a battle at Otford.

67 This was the second Baron Howard of Effingham (1536–1624) who as Lord High Admiral commanded the fleet against the Armada in 1588 (see G. Mattingly, *The Defeat of the Spanish Armada*, 1959, p. 289f). He was created Earl of Nottingham in 1597. It was his father, the first Baron (1510?–73) who was granted the Priory by Henry VIII in 1541. Of this house little survives. See *B. of E. Surrey*, pp. 361–3.

68 This priory was founded in 1235 for Augustinian Canons and was dissolved in 1535. Little of it remains. *B. of E. Surrey*, pp. 360–61.

69 William, who died in 1240. His father Hamelin, an illegitimate son of Geoffrey Plantagenet, married the Warenne heiress Isabel and acquired their title by right of his wife (p. 25, n. 88).

70 Only an earthwork motte and bailey and a sham gatehouse of C18 are to be seen now. It was established by the William de Warenne (d. 1088) who fought at Hastings (p. 24, n. 78) and it was slighted in 1648. See *B. of E. Surrey*, p. 360f., for castle and town.

71 These tunnels were probably made in quarrying for sand and may later have been used as cellars. On the origins of Reigate, see *New Towns*, p. 491.

72 Probably the *Inquisitions Post Mortem* which were 'inquiries into the land held by a tenant in chief at his death'. *Public Records*, p. 43. For other kinds of royal enquiries see *Oxf. Hist.* IV, 358–60.

73 Betchworth. The site of the castle, of which little survived its demolition in early C18, is over a mile west of the very pleasant village. *B. of E. Surrey*, pp. 93–4.

74 Sir Anthony Browne (1526–92), see n. 76 below.

75 John Neville (d. 1471), Marquis of Montagu, was rewarded by Edward IV with the lands and earldom of Northumberland as a result of his victory at Hexham in 1464. When these lands and the title were restored to Henry Percy, Neville changed sides and was killed at Barnet in 1471 fighting for the Lancastrians.

76 So created in 1554, he was a Catholic who nevertheless was faithful to both Edward VI and Elizabeth. His principal seat was at Cowdray, Sussex (p. 58, n. 55).

77 Effingham has been suburbanized to such an extent in the last 40 years that almost all its character as a village has gone. Only its common survives unscathed.

78 William, Lord Howard of Effingham (1510?–73) became Lord Admiral in 1553, Lord Chamberlain in 1558 and Lord Privy Seal in 1572. He was engaged in the defence of London against the rebels led by Wyatt in 1554. *Oxf. Hist.* VII, 538.

Betchworth Castle, engraved by Hay after J. Loch, published in 1811

which it stands. Under it I saw an extraordinary passage with a vaulted roof hewn with great labor out of the soft stone of which the hill is composed.[71] "The earls of Warren," as we find in the "book of Inquisitions,[72] held it in chief of the king in their barony from the conquest of England." Thence the river runs by *Bechworth* castle,[73] for which Thomas *Brown* procured a fair of Henry VI. It is the residence of the knightly family of the Browns, of whom two centuries ago Anthony Brown [74] marrying Lucy, 4th daughter of John Neville marquis Monta-cute,[75] with a large fortune, his grandson was vested with the title of viscount *Montacute* [76] by queen Mary. A few miles west[s] from hence is *Effingham*,[77] some time since the property of William Howard [78] (son of Thomas duke of Norfolk, who defeated the Scots) [79] created by queen Mary baron *Howard* of *Effingham*, and high admiral of England, first chamberlain, and afterwards keeper of the privy seal to queen Elizabeth of glorious memory, whose son Charles is now high admiral of England,[80] and was in 1597, for his valor and signal services,

g. N.W.

79 Thomas Howard (1443–1524), Earl of Surrey (1483) and second of the Howards to become Duke of Norfolk (1514), was given the office of Lord Treasurer in 1501 and Earl Marshal in 1510. He defeated the Scots at Flodden in 1513. See *Oxf. Hist.* VII, 279–83.

80 See n. 67 above.

Kingston Market Place, engraved by J. Greig after I. Hassal,
published in 1811

created by the same princess earl of Nottingham.[h] But to return
to the river.

The Mole coming to a hill called from its colour *White hill*,[82]
producing plenty of box, hides itself, or rather is swallowed up
at its foot, whence the place has the name of the *Swallow*,[83] and
after about a mile or two bubbles up again near *Letherhed*
bridge:[84] so that the inhabitants of this place boast that they
have a bridge which feeds sheep,[85] as well as the Spaniards;
among whom this is a trite proverb of the place where the river
Anas, now Guadiana, hides itself for ten miles. Our Mole thus
risen again moves slowly on to the Thames, into which it falls
above *Molesey*[86] called after its name.

Thames after receiving the Mole rolls its waters due north,
passing by *Kingstone*, antiently as some say called *Moreford*,[87] a
considerable market town,[88] formerly remarkable for a castle

h. Of whom more in my annals. H.[81]

81 This is a footnote added by
Thomas Hearne (p. 27, n. 37, *Kent*)
referring the reader to his edition of
Camden's *Annales*, published in
1717.

82 This must be Box Hill of which
the name is first recorded in 1629,
though there are c13 personal names
which probably referred to the same

place (*P.N. Surrey*, p. 270). Box-trees
are still numerous there and many
flowering plants in spite of excessive
use by week-end crowds. See J. E.
Lousley, *Wild Flowers of Chalk and
Limestone*, 1950, pp. 17–48. White
Hill (or Downs) is further west.

83 'Swallow', in this sense, is from
Old English *swealwe*, 'a whirlpool,

rushing water', which is the origin
of the river-name Swale (Berks.,
Kent and Yorks.), as well as
Swallow, Lincs.

84 See p. 10, n. 56. The present
bridge dates essentially from 1782.

85 The point of this anecdote seems
to be that the dry river bed provided
a crossing that obviated use of the
bridge, which consequently became
sufficiently grass-grown to feed
sheep. Gibson (ed. 1695, p. 156),
however, sees the matter a little
differently. Flocks of sheep are
pastured over the course of the
underground river.

86 Molesey is now a dreary spot.
See p. 10, n. 57.

87 I find no mention elsewhere of
this name nor apparently did Gough
(*Additions*, p. 176) and earlier editors.

88 A much-diminished cattle market
survived the Second World War for
only a few years, for pastures are
now increasingly distant from the
town. The Monday Market still
survives in 1975. Much of this town
has been disfigured by the 'im-
prover's' hand, but the Market
Place has some attractive groupings
of older shops and the whole has
character far beyond that which the
twentieth century can achieve. In his
scanty notes for Surrey, Leland
(*L.T.S.* iv, 85) says this of the town:

The olde monuments of the town of
Kingeston be founde yn the declyving
doune [descent] from Come [Combe]
parke towards the galoys [gallows,
c. NG 195705]; and there yn ploughyng
and digging have very often beene
founde fundation of waulles of houses,
and diverse coynes of brasse, sylver and
gold, with Romaine inscriptions, and
paintid yerthen pottes; and yn one in the
Cardinal Wolsey's tyme was found
much Romayne mony of sylver, and
plates of silver to coyne, and masses to
bete into plates to coyne, and [chay]nes
of sylver. And yn the old tyme the
commune saying ys that the bridge,
where the commune passage was over
the Tamise at olde Kingston, was lower

13

on the ryver then it is now. And when men began the new town yn the Saxons tymes they toke from the very clyve [steep slope] of Come parke side to builde on the Tamise side: and sette a new bridge hard by the same. The tounisch men of Kingston contend that wher their toun chirche is now was sumtyme an abbay. But I se no likelihod of it. For King Henry the Second did appropriate their chirch as a paroche chirche, not as abbay, priory or celle, to Marten [Merton] Abbay in Southerey [Surrey]. The tounisch men have certen knowlege of a few kinges crounid ther afore the Conqueste; and contende that 2. or 3. kinges were buried yn their paroche chirch; but they can not bring no profe nor likelihod of it. In the new toune by the Tamise side there is a house yet caullid the Bisshopes Haulle. But now it is turnid into a commune dwellinge house of a tounisch man. It was sumtyme the Bisshop of Winchester's house: and as far as I can conject sum bisshop, wery of it, did neglect this house, and began to build at Assher [Esher] nere the Tamise side 2. or 3. miles above Kingeston. Dyverse kinges have given great privileges to the town of Kingeston, as it is yn this tyme. And Kingston is the beste market [towne of] all Southerey. Ther was (and is a chapelle) at Kingeston caullid Magdalenes, to the which is yoinid an hospitale, wheryn was a master, 2. prestes, and certen poore men, and the maker of it was one Lofkin ['fishemonger and maior of London', adds John Stow], mayre, as I hard, of London: and this man, as I harde, was borne in Kingston self, and dwellid in Tamise Streat about New Fisch Streate; and that he was founder of the college of the chirch of St Michaelles by Crokid Lane. And, as I can gesse, this Lofkyn dwellid there in the house that Mr. Finkel dwellid yn, and was buried yn the body of S. Michael's church. These 3. chapelles and hammes lying on the Tames side from Kingston toward London, that is Peter Ham, Richemont or Shene, and Kew longe [belong] to Kingeston, and so up almost to Mortela[ke]. And the privilege of Kingeston strechith upward almost to Cobham.

89 Gilbert de Clare (1243–95), ninth Earl of Clare, seventh Earl of Hertford and eighth Earl of

of the *Clares* earls of Gloucester,[89] which rose out of an older little town of the same name, lying low and subject to floods, in which when England was almost torn in pieces by the Danish wars, Ethelstan,[i] Edwin,[k] and Ethelred,[l] were crowned;[93] whence it had the name of *Kingston* or *Kings-town*. In this neighbourhood our kings since chose their residence, called from its splendor [94] *Shene*,* now *Richmond*, where that potent monarch Edward III. when he had filled up the measure of his glory and life, ended his days with grief for the loss of his brave son, irreparable both to him and the nation.[95] If ever England had cause to mourn, it certainly was at that time. For in one year she lost the substantial glory of military atchievements and accomplished valour: both princes by carrying their victorious arms through France had inspired such dread of them that the father might dispute the title of Thunderer with Antiochus,[96] and the son, that of the Eagle with Pyrrhus.[97]

i. A.D. 425.[90]   k. A.D. 455.[91]   l. A.D. 948.[92]

*Both the place and village of Richmond were called *Shene* before the time of Henry VII.

Gloucester, held Kingston for the barons during the de Montfort rebellion and it was captured by Henry III in 1264. A Clare castle here could only have been a temporary, makeshift one; but perhaps Camden had in mind a building called King John's Palace or Dairy (NG 178690), which was demolished in 1805 and of which a tradition goes back to early C13. A stone column said to have come from the site is preserved outside the Public Library.

90 Correctly A.D. 925.

91 This must be the Eadwig crowned in 955.

92 In 978.

93 Probably six Saxon kings, Athelstan (925), Edmund (939), Eadred (946), Eadwig (955), Edward the Martyr (975) and Ethelred II (978) were crowned here. The place was called Kingston because it was a royal manor (*P.N. Surrey*, p. 59).

Camden's 'Kingstone' may be a form influenced by the knowledge of the reputed Saxon coronation stone there.

94 Camden's explanation of the meaning of Sheen was endorsed, somewhat hesitantly (*P.N. Surrey*, pp. 65–6), until recently; but *Elements* II, 107, derives this name from Old English *scēo*, 'a shelter'.

95 Edward III died in 1377; his son, the Black Prince, some months earlier in 1376.

96 Greek Βρόντης had a normal meaning 'Thunderer' and a derived sense 'irresistible conqueror', but none of the thirteen kings of Syria called Antiochus could be so described nor, for the whole of his career, could Edward III.

97 Pyrrhus (318–272 B.C.), King of Epirus, successfully waged war against both the Romans and the Carthaginians.

Richmond Palace in 1638, engraved by Wenceslaus Hollar

Here likewise died Anne[98] wife of Richard II. sister of the emperor Wenceslaus, daughter of the emperor Charles III. who first taught the English women the present method of sitting on horseback, before which they rode in an indecent manner like the men astride.[99] Her husband laid her death so much to heart that he forsook and loathed the house. Henry V. embellished it with new buildings, and founded in the neighbouring village of *Shene* a small monastery for Carthusians which he called *Bethlehem*.[01] In the reign of Henry VII. this palace was entirely destroyed by fire;[02] but by the assistance of that prince it rose like a phœnix out of its ashes with greater splendor,[03] and received the new name of Richmond[04] from the county from whence he took the title of earl before his accession to the crown. This prince, by whose care, vigilance, councils, and prudent foresight the state of England still subsists unshaken, had scarce put the finishing hand to this house when he died in it. From this place also (30 years after)[05] his grandaughter, our gracious queen Elizabeth, full of years, being near 70, was called by Heaven to the assembly of the blessed:[06] a princess of a manly spirit and discernment, resembling her royal grandfather in disposition as well as in features, the love of the world, and the delight of Britain. Though a woman, she was so far from degenerating from the continued and renowned virtue of her ancestors that she came up to them if she did not surpass them. Let the latest posterity believe this, and that so gracious a lady (for I scorn to debase the truth by flattery) swayed the sceptre 44 years in such a manner as to be loved by

98 Anne of Bohemia was his first wife who died in 1394 of the plague.

99 'The custom of riding side-saddle did not spread in England before the latter part of the fourteenth century, and even then it was not general.' *English Wayfaring Life*, p. 50.

01 Founded in 1414; site NG 171758.

02 In 1497.

03 See pl. 18 in *B. of E. Surrey* for a view of the palace in c. 1500. The surviving gatehouse has the arms of Henry VII in much decayed stone. Beside the gate is a building of C18 into which some Tudor walling was incorporated. The gatehouse faces on to Richmond Green, the original place for jousting. This 'is one of the most beautiful urban greens surviving anywhere in England' (*B. of E. Surrey*, pp. 369–70). Surrounding it on two sides are groups of mainly eighteenth-century houses of delightful quality in all.

04 In the North Riding of Yorkshire around the town of Richmond, itself named from one of the Richemonts in France. *Dic.*, p. 368.

05 (30 years after) should be (94 years after).

06 But not from the surviving gatehouse as tradition sometimes has it.

07 The tide now reaches to Teddington Lock and would go farther but for that barrier. As south-eastern England has been sinking relative to the sea at a rate of 6 to 12 inches each century since Roman times, the tide has penetrated gradually farther up the Thames and other rivers. See e.g. R. E. M. Wheeler, *London in Roman Times*, 1930, pp. 12–13, and *The Personality of Britain*, p. 24f.

08 The same as the ancient Roman mile of 1000 paces (*mille passuum*) equivalent to about 1618 yards. *Antiquity* XXXII, 52.

09 The House of Valois, in one or other of its branches, ruled France from 1328 to 1589.

10 'Wain' here is modern 'wane' (decline in size) and 'wear' is used in a specialized sense, 'go, advance' (*S.O.E.D.*, p. 2399, VI). The whole phrase implies moving across the sky and waning concurrently.

11 The Palace (NG 228631) was begun in 1538 and demolition began in 1682. For a description, plan and drawing of it see *B. of E. Surrey*, pp. 124–7 and pl. 19. The foundations of the banqueting house remain visible (NG 224628), but little else besides earthworks. See J. Dent, *The Quest for Nonsuch*, 1962, and M. Biddle, *Surrey Arch. Coll.* LVIII.

12 The village of Cuddington was destroyed to make way for the Palace. During its excavation the foundations of the church and some of the villagers' graves were discovered.

13 The very name 'Nonsuch' implied that Henry aimed to exceed other palaces in splendour and cost. It was largely French in manner and the craftsmen were mostly foreigners.

14 This is presumably from Leland's *Cygnea Cantio*. See Appendix.

her subjects, feared by her enemies, and admired by all; an example unparalleled in former times. Her death occasioned such universal sorrow in England that the nation would have sunk under the expressions of its grief inconsolable had not, immediately upon her removal from the world, our most gracious sovereign James, the true and undisputed heir to the crown in the eyes and by the wishes of all, shone out upon us with his most august beams, and called us to the hope of enjoying him for ever. While we behold *him* we forget that *she* is gone. Yet how can we say she is gone when her immortal virtues live, and her deathless fame will survive for ever in the minds of men through endless ages.

Thus far the tide 07 comes up the Thames about 60 Italian miles 08 from its mouth. Nor do I know any other river in Europe that receives the influx of the ocean with a regular succession of tides for so many miles to the great benefit of the people on its banks. Whether this arises as I once thought from its having so little bend hereabouts, and proceeding with a strait course eastward, confined for the most part within steeper banks, and emptying itself with a wider mouth than most rivers into the sea, which by the revolution of the heavenly bodies from east to west is driven in the same direction, philosophers must determine, and to their discussion I resign this and all such points. A few lines on this place and this subject from the marriage of the Thame and Isis may not perhaps be disagreeable to the reader:

> *A dextra nobis Richmondia, Shena vetustis,*
> *Celsa nitet, sapiens namque hanc Richmondia dici*
> *Henricus voluit, sibi quod retulisset honorem*
> *Et titulos comitis Richmondia jure paterno.*
> *Hectoris Edwardi sed deflet funera nostri:*
> *Proh dolor! hic illi regi mens libera cessit*
> *Corpore contempto, sedes habitura supernas:*
> *Quem si non subito rapuissent ferrea fata,*
> *Aut te Valesiis rapuisset Gallia victor,*
> *Aut tibi Valesios.*

> Now to the right is lofty Richmond seen,
> Call'd in past ages from its lustre *Shene*.
> Its modern name to that sage prince it owes
> Whose antient style and title that name shows:
> It lasting tribute to our Hector pays,
> Edward the Third, who ended here his days.

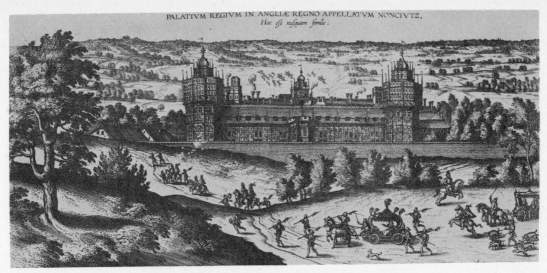

Nonsuch Palace in 1582, engraved by Joris Hoefnagel

His godlike soul from hence to heav'n return'd
Free from the mortal fetters which it spurn'd.
Victorious Edward died, e'er to their cost
Or Valois, France, or France had Valois lost.[09]

and a few lines after,

Tamesis alternum sentit reditumque fugamque
Huc reflui pelagi: quoties vaga Cynthia pronos
Octava librat cœli statione jugales,
Aut tenet oppositam varianti lumine plagam,
Plenior increscit, celeremque recurrit in æstum;
Atque superbus ait, Concedant flumina nobis:
Nulla per Europæ dotatas nomine terras
Flumina tam longe sic certis legibus undas
Alternas renovant, nisi fratres Scaldis & Albis.

Oft as the changing moon the ocean wide
Impels, our Thames receives the changing tide;
When in mid heaven fair Cynthia glorious rides
By her directed onwards rush the tides.
When on the other side she wears in wain[10]
The tides attendant hasten back again;
By force acquir'd the exulting river swell'd
Rolls on, and cries, "To me all rivers yield:"
Save the twin brother floods of Elbe and Scheld.
With such true tides no river can be found
In all the realms that Europe's empire bound.

15 The twelfth earl (1511?–80), godson of Henry VIII and lord chamberlain to him and to Edward VI. He was buried at Arundel. See *B. of E. Sussex*, p. 89.

16 This seems to be John (1534?–1609), first baron of the second creation, whose monument and those of others of the family are in the Lumley Chapel at Cheam, close to Nonsuch. On this family see p. 42, n. 17.

17 A plastic clay relatively free from iron compounds. Leland (*L.T.S.* IV, 121):

Compton of London hath a close by Codington [Cuddington] in Southerey where the King buildith. In this close is a vaine of fine yerth [earth] to make moldes for goldesmithes and casters of metale that a loode [load] of it is solde for 2. crounes of golde. Like yerth to this is [not] found yet in al Englande.

18 No longer clear, but in its lower reaches a nasty industrial sewer. For its earlier industrialization see *Surrey Arch. Coll.* XXI, 170f.

19 The spring-ponds of the Wandle at Carshalton, with some of the surrounding houses, are a delightful amenity.

20 Merton is apparently from Old English *mere-tūn.* 'farm by a pool', and a form in *-dūne* (hill) as cited by Camden is erroneous. There is no hill there. See *P.N. Surrey*, p. 25.

21 The 'identification of Merton with *Meretun* where Cynewulf... was staying when he met his death is exceedingly doubtful' (*P.N. Surrey*, p. 25). Merton was in Mercian territory from before 675 until early c9 and the *Anglo-Saxon Chronicle* places the event under the year 755 (which should be 757, p. 29, n. 11). Cynewulf was slain in 786. See *Two Saxon Chrons.* II, 44–7, and *Oxf. Hist.* II, 208, n.

22 Clito here means 'prince' or 'aetheling', from the Greek κλῦτός, 'glorious, renowned'.

23 Merton Priory, founded in 1117 and built for Augustinian canons from 1130, was robbed of its stone for the building of Nonsuch Palace. Much of its site lies under the railway, but a gateway of c16 and some walling survive in Merton Abbey Station Road on the south side, and parts of a Norman doorway were removed in 1935 to the parish churchyard. *B. of E. Surrey*, p. 309.

24 At a meeting of the Great Council in 1236 the attempt of King and Church to enforce Canon Law for the legitimization of children born before marriage was resisted successfully. Among other sections of the Statute of Merton was that permitting a lord to enclose waste land provided that sufficient common land remained. *Oxf. Hist.* IV, 69.

25 No such 'antient' form as *Cradiden* appears to have been worthy of the attention of the scholars of the English Place-Name Survey (*P.N. Surrey*, pp. 47–8); indeed, it is far from the *Crogedene* of early MSS, which represent its true form. It meant 'valley where saffron grows'.

26 In its present form the Palace is mainly of c14 and 15. See *B. of E.*

About four miles inland from the Thames all the surrounding buildings are eclipsed by *Nonesuch*,[11] a royal retreat chosen by the magnificent monarch Henry VIII. for his pleasure and retirement, in a most healthy spot before called *Cuddington*,[12] and built with so much splendor and elegance that it stands a monument of art, and you would think the whole science of architecture exhausted on this building. It has such a profusion of animated statues and finished pieces of art rivalling the monuments of antient Rome itself,[13] that it justly has and maintains its name from them, as Leland sings,

> *Hanc quia non habeant similem, laudare Britanni*
> *Sepe solent,* Nullique parem *cognomine dicunt.*

> Unrivall'd in design the Britons tell
> The wond'rous praises of this *Nonpareil.*[14]

The house is so surrounded by parks full of deer, delicious gardens, artificial arbours, parterres, and shady walks, that it seems the spot where pleasure chose to dwell with health. Queen Mary exchanged it for other estates with Henry *Fitz-Alan* earl of Arundel,[15] who added to it a well-furnished library and new buildings, leaving it at his death to lord *Lumley*,[16] who left nothing undone that should make it answer its name,[m] and of him it has been since purchased by the crown. Near it, I should just observe, is a vein of potters earth,[17] excellent for making crucibles for goldsmiths, and sold at a high price.

The clear little river *Wandle*,[18] full of excellent trouts, rises not far from hence at *Cashalton*,[19] and passing by *Morden* leaves on its west bank *Merton*,[20] situate in a most fruitful spot, and called by the Saxons 'Meredune', antiently famous [21] for the death of Kinulphus king of the West Saxons, killed here by Kinehard Clito [22] in the small hut of an insignificant harlot, of whom he was violently enamoured: Kinehard himself was afterwards slain by the friends of Kinulph; and thus suffered the instant punishment of his treachery. At present this place shews only the ruins of a monastery,[23] founded by Henry I. at the instigation of Gilbert sheriff of Surrey, and famous for the parliament held at it under Henry III.[24]

m. Gibson mistakes *suo nomini* [in Camden's Latin], which obviously belongs to the *house.*

Surrey, pp. 160–61. The building is not especially interesting from

the outside. See *Arch. Journ.* CXXVII, 133–8, with plans.

18

Croydon Palace, engraved after N. Whittock, published in 1829

The Wandle is afterwards increased from the east by a little stream rising at *Croydon*, antiently *Cradiden*,[25] situate under the hills, and remarkable for the palace of the archbishops of Canterbury,[26] to whom it has long belonged, and for the trade which the inhabitants carry on in coals.[27] They say here was once a royal palace in the west part of the town near *Haling*,[28] where foundations are frequently dug up, which was afterwards given by the kings to the archbishops,[29] who removed it to their own palace nearer the river. Near this the most reverend father in Christ John *Whitgift*,[30] late archbishop of Canterbury of famous memory, piously founded and endowed a very handsome hospital[31] for the relief of the poor, and a school[32] for the advancement of learning. It may seem hardly worth while to mention, though not absolutely void of truth, that a brook here is said by the common people to swell sometimes suddenly, betokening scarcity or plague.[33] A little way from hence is *Beddington*, where we see a beautiful house[34] and delightful garden, lately built and laid out by Sir Francis *Carew*,[35] knight. This is the antient seat of the Carews who are

29 The manor of Croydon was presented to Archbishop Lanfranc by William the Conqueror.

30 He was archbishop from 1583 to 1604, much favoured by Elizabeth who nicknamed him her 'little black husband'. His alabaster tomb is in Croydon parish church. *B. of E. Surrey*, p. 158.

31 This was built in 1596–9 and Camden's reference to it was added after the publication of the first edition of *Britannia* in 1586. The hospital survives largely in its original form. Details in *B. of E. Surrey*, p. 165. Much of its quality is lost through its situation at a dangerous and noisy crossroad.

32 The original buildings of the school were destroyed in C19.

33 The 'Bourne...appears only at intervals of from 5 to 7 years, and then only for short periods. Rising in Marden Park (NG c. 360550)...it flows through Caterham to Croydon, over what is usually arable land, and joins the head of the Wandle at Waddon (NG c. 310650)'. *Surrey Arch. Coll.* XXI, 171. This is a Winterbourne (i.e. a stream dry except in winter), flowing intermittently after sustained rainfall when the water-table in the chalk (as at Croydon) rises above the level of the valley floor. Such streams gave name to villages in Dorset, Berks., Wilts. and the West Riding.

34 Of this house (NG 288653), the Great Hall with a very fine roof (c. 1530–40) survives. *B. of E. Surrey*, p. 91.

35 His monument (1611) is in the church with those of some of his ancestors: Sir Nicholas, d. 1432 (a brass) and Sir Richard, d. 1520. Another Sir Nicholas was beheaded in 1539 for treason. For the brass see *Monumental Brasses*, pl. 17, and for the rest, see *B. of E. Surrey*, p. 90. It is strange that Camden makes no mention here of the Cornish Carews, another branch of the

27 This refers to charcoal. Mined coal was usually referred to as sea-coal in Camden's day. *Grim, the Collier of Croydon*, published in 1600, was a popular play. See E. Parker, *Highways and Byways, East and Central Surrey*, 1937, p. 362, and *Hist. Geog. Eng.*, p. 227 and references there.

28 As this had been a royal manor, the manor house could presumably be called a palace. Nothing remains of it.

19

family. Sir Richard Carew of Antony was his almost life-long friend and author of the *Survey of Cornwall*, published in 1602. See the edition of 1969, p.62, and above p.xxii.

36 Of them Camden says: '...the Thames flows...through Moulesford [Berks. NG 590840], which Henry I. gave to Giraldus Fitz Walter, from whom is descended the noble family of Carew, who derive much honour from their marriage with the noble family of Mohun, Dinham, and others, both in Ireland and England' (Gough edn, p.149).

37 See p.61, n.90.

38 The place at which the battle of A.D. 568 occurred, according to the *Anglo-Saxon Chronicle*, cannot be Wimbledon, the earliest forms of which strongly suggest '*Wynnmann's* hill'. *P.N. Surrey*, p.38, and *P.N. Herts*, 1958, p.xlii.

39 This king (560?–616) was baptized by St Augustine in 597, the first English king to be converted. See p.48, n.16, *Kent*.

40 *Ceawlin* (560–91) was king of the *West* Saxons.

41 This should be Oslaf (or Oslac in MSS 'E' and 'F' of the *Chronicle*) and Cnebban; but Cneben, which is not found in the original source, suited Camden better in his false derivation of Bensbury (n.43 immediately below).

42 Excavations in 1937 showed the fort (NG 224710) to have been the work of Early Iron Age immigrants, probably of C3 B.C. See *Arch. Journ.* CII, 15f. These earthworks were much damaged by 'developers' in late C19, but their outline is traceable if one braves the missiles of the golfers who are in possession.

43 The only early form found of this name is *bæncesbyri* (*P.N. Surrey*, p.12, n.1), which remains unexplained. 'Bensbury' is a normal development from the older form; 'Cnebensbury' is most improbable.

20

Croydon Church in 1770, engraved by Godfrey after Francis Grose

descended from Nicholas lord *Carew* of *Moulesford* [36] (from whom also the *Carews* of Devonshire are derived) and have long flourished in this county, but especially since James Carew married the daughter and coheiress of the most noble baron Hoo.[37] *Wibbandune*,[38] now commonly called *Wimbledon*, stands on the other bank of the Wandle, where, when long prosperity had produced civil wars among the Saxons after their wars with the Britans were ended, Ethelbert[39] king of

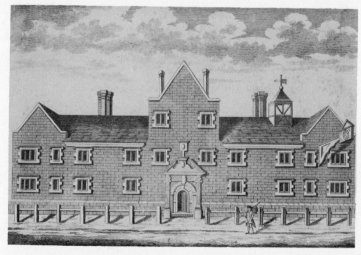

Croydon, Archbishop Whitgift's Hospital in 1755, engraved by J. Royce after F. Perry

Kent first sounded the alarm against his countrymen: but Ceaulin,[40] king of the East Saxons, fortunately defeated him here with great slaughter,[n] having slain his generals Oslan and Cneben,[41] from which last probably the circular fortification[42] to be seen here was called *Bensbury* for *Cnebensbury*.[43] At present this place is embellished with a fine house[44] having pleasant gardens and prospects, built by Sir Thomas Cecil,[45] knight, son of the wise lord Burghley, in 1588, when the Spanish fleet was preparing to invade England.

Two miles south from hence on the top of a hill is a little wood, now called *Woodcote*,[46] in which are evident traces of a

Wimbledon House, begun 1588 and demolished c. 1720

small town, and several wells formed of flints, and the neighbours talk much of its populousness, and wealth and many nobles. This was, in my opinion, the city called by Ptolemy NOIOMAGUS, by Antoninus NOVIOMAGUS;[47] nor have I any other authority for my conjecture except the distance; it being 10 miles from London, 18 from *Vaginiacæ* according to the old Itinerary.[48] They, therefore, who place *Noviomagus* at *Buckingham*[o] or *Guilford*[p] are very wide of the mark. This was the capital of the REGNI,[51] and known to the old geographer

n. A.D. 568.
o. George Lilly in his book of the names of antient places.[49]
p. H. Lluid, Fragm. Brit.[50]

44 This was the manor-house long since lost. See pp. 36–7 of *Architecture in Britain, 1530–1830*.

45 'Wise lord Burghley' began building Wimbledon House in 1588. His son Thomas (1542–1623) succeeded to the Barony of Burghley in 1598 and was created Earl of Exeter in 1605.

46 The evidence of Roman occupation found here (?NG c. 290610) is insufficient for a town. See *Archaeology of Surrey*, pp. 138, 223.

47 One settlement called *Noviomagus* in Roman times was probably at Crayford, Kent. *Vaginiacæ* was probably at Springhead, a few miles to the east along the Roman road later called Watling Street. The capital of the *Regenses* was also called *Noviomagus*; Chichester overlies it. See O.S. *Map of Roman Britain*, p. 27, and n. 51 immediately below. For a history of speculation concerning the site of this *Noviomagus* see *Antiquaries Journal* XXVII, 1947, p. 183f.

48 The *Antonine Itinerary* is a routebook for the Roman Empire, with distances between places stated route by route. It was probably compiled during the reign of the Emperor Caracalla (A.D. 211–17) whose proper name was Marcus Aurelius Antoninus. The *Itinerary* was amended and added to later. The British Section is given as a map in the O.S. *Map of Roman Britain*, p. 21.

49 Lilly (d. 1559) was a canon of Canterbury and author of some historical works in Latin.

50 Humphrey Llwyd (1527–68) was an author of antiquarian works including *Commentarioli Descriptionis Britannicae Fragmentum*, 1572. On this short work see *British Antiquity*, pp. 136–7.

51 Ptolemy (p. 1, n. 02) calls this tribe the *Regni* and their capital *Noviomagus*; but the *Itinerary* refers to the town as *Regnum*. The tribe is now usually referred to as 'the

Regnenses, or people of the native kingdom' (*regnum*). *Roman Britain*, p. 23. See also n. 47 immediately above.

52 Marinus of Tyre (CI) was a main source of information for Ptolemy, on whom see p. 1, n. 02.

53 Wandsworth means '*Wændel*'s enclosure or farm'. The settlement gave its name to the river and not vice versa as Camden says. An earlier name of the river was *hlidaburna*, 'noisy stream'. *P.N. Surrey*, pp. 7, 12, n. 1; and see *B. of E. London* II, 433 f.

54 Battersea means '*Beadurīc*'s marshy island (*ēg*)'. *P.N. Surrey*, pp. 13–14. Some early spellings of this place-name, e.g. *Patricesy*, 1086, do reveal a confusion with the name (St) Patrick. The parish church (rebuilt in 1776) is however dedicated to St Mary and not to St Patrick. The personal name *Beadurīc* is nevertheless rare enough to have made the substitution of a familiar name a strong temptation. See *B. of E. London* II, 49 f.

55 The name Kennington survives unchanged from Camden's day, meaning '*Cæna*'s farm (*tūn*)'. *P.N. Surrey*, p. 23; and see *B. of E. London* II, 284.

56 The Black Prince's Palace (c. 1340 and later), demolished in 1531, was rediscovered by excavations from 1965 to 1967. See *Med. Arch.* XI, 1967, pp. 296–7, with a plan, and the *London Archaeologist*, Winter 1968, pp. 6–8, for a fuller account.

57 Lambeth meant 'the landing-place (*hȳth*) for lambs'. *P.N. Surrey*, p. 22. Spellings of C14, such as *Lomheth(e)*, instances of the rounding of the 'a' sound to 'o' (ibid., p. xxiv), may have misled Camden into thinking that the first element of this place-name was the word 'loam' (OE *lām*) rather than *lamb*.

58 The *Chronicle*, MS 'E', under the year 1041 (correctly 1042) reads: 'In this year Harthacnut died at

Lambeth Palace in 1647, engraved by Wenceslaus Hollar

Marinus Tyrius,[52] whom Ptolemy calls to account for placing *Noviomagus* in Britain more north than London in climate, and more south by distance of roads.

On the Thames below the mouth of the Wandle, on which stands the little town of *Wandlesworth*,[53] which has its name from it, is *Batersey*[54] a small village, antiently called by the Saxons 'Patryks-ea' or *Patrick's isle*; and the royal palace of *Kennington* not now to be found, the retreat of our antient kings, but now both name[55] and ruins[56] are lost. Next to this is *Lambith* or *Lomehith*, q.d. the muddy station or harbour,[57] famous for the death of Hardicanute king of England,[58] who died suddenly while drinking.[q] Fond of festivity and good living "he made," says Huntingdon,[59] "four royal dinners a

q. At the wedding of Osgod the Dane, lord of the place. [See n. 58.]

Lambeth on 8th June; he was king of all England for two years. . . .' MS 'C' adds: he 'died as he stood at his drink and he suddenly fell to the ground with a terrible convulsion . . .'. The *Chronicle* makes no reference at this point to Osgod the Dane (Gough's note *q*) who was nicknamed *Clapa*, 'the goggle-eyed'. This comes from the later source, Florence of Worcester (d. 1118), the author of *Chronicon ex Chronicis* which goes down to 1117. This work was continued by other chroniclers to 1295. It was first edited by Lord William Howard in 1592. Florence is original only where he interpolates contemporary matter of his

own lifetime. His main sources are Bede and the *Anglo-Saxon Chronicle*. See *Camb. Hist. Eng. Lit.* I, 161–2; *Oxf. Hist.* II, 682; and for a translation of select passages, *E.H.D.* II, 204 f. Florence states that Harthacnut died 'at the feast which Osgod Clapa was giving in honour of the marriage of his daughter Gytha to Tofig the Proud . . .'. *Two Saxon Chrons.* II, 221.

59 Henry of Huntingdon (1084?–1155) continued his *Historia Anglorum* to the year of his death. He is inferior to William of Malmesbury (d. 1143?) as a reliable historian. On the Latin chroniclers of this period see *Camb. Hist. Eng. Lit.* I, 156–82.

day for his whole court, chusing rather that his guests should neglect a dinner ready dressed than be always demanding a dinner to be dressed." The place is at present more remarkable for the palace[60] of the archbishops of Canterbury. About the year 1183 Baldwin, archbishop of Canterbury,[61] purchased it by exchange with the bishop of Rochester, and began a palace for himself and successors, who gradually enlarged it. But attempting to establish a collegiate church here, innumerable appeals were dispatched to Rome from the monks of Canterbury,[62] and as many thunders, threats, and censures were discharged at the archbishop by the Pope. The monks were dreadfully afraid it should prove the ruin of their support, and invade their right of electing the archbishops. Nor could the storm be laid till the monks by their instances procured the little church to be levelled with the ground. Near this is that most famous market town in the county called now the *Borough of Southworke*, by the Saxons 'Suthwerke', q.d. the *Southern work* or *building*,[63] from its south situation opposite to London, of which it seems a kind of suburb, but so large and populous as not to be inferior to many cities in England, having in some measure its own liberties, and in the last age its own bailiffs; but being united to London under Edward VI. it is now considered as part of it.[64] We shall therefore say more of it when we come to London.

Below this the Thames leaves Surrey, whose eastern boundary runs hence due south towards *Lagham*,[65] which t. Edward I. had its own barons summoned to parliament by the style of *St. John de Lagham*, whose estates passed afterwards by a daughter and heiress to J   Leodiard.[r] Lower in the angle towards Sussex and Kent is *Sterborrow* castle,[66] formerly the seat of the lords *Cobham*, who from it take the title of *Sterborrow*, and descending from John de *Cobham*[67] lord of *Cobham* and *Couling* by a daughter of Hugh Neville, long flourished there. Reginald[68] made a knight of the Garter by Edward III. was admiral of the coast from the mouth of the Thames eastward. The last of them Thomas married Anne, daughter of the duke of Buckingham, and had by her an only daughter Anne,

r. This is a mistake.

60 The Palace fronts the Thames (NG 305791) with a brick gatehouse of c. 1495, a water-tower of 1435, Cranmer's tower of mid-C16 and a splendid great hall of c. 1660. The chapel and its undercroft are of early C13 and the north range of the cloister is medieval too. See *B. of E. London* II, 281–3 and pl. 2a, 16b.

61 Baldwin, who died in 1190, had been abbot of the Cistercian house at Ford in Devonshire and bishop of Worcester.

62 Baldwin charged them with easy and luxurious living. See also p. 51, n. 40, *Kent*.

63 The original etymology of this name is 'the defensive work (*geweorc*) of the men of Surrey (*Suthrigea*)'. *P.N. Surrey*, pp. 29–30. Later, as Camden says, it is 'the south work' in relation to Old London Bridge.

64 See *Survey of London, 1598*, p. 358f., for details of Southwark in Camden's day.

65 Lagham in Godstone parish has an extensive moated site surviving from the Middle Ages.

66 Starborough Castle in Lingfield parish retains only the moat and fragments of the gatehouse. Begun in c. 1341 by Reginald de Cobham, it bore some resemblance to Bodiam Castle (p. 66, n. 29). It was demolished during the Civil War of C17. The tomb of Reginald, Lord Cobham of Sterborough (d. 1361) is in Lingfield church (*B. of E. Surrey*, pl. 14, pp. 390–91).

67 A brass to John de Cobham (d. 1299) formerly existed in the church at Cobham, Kent. There are still the memorial brasses of nine other Cobhams there. See *Monumental Brasses*, pl. 14. As a whole, this is the finest group of brasses anywhere. See pp. 14–15, nn. 19, 21 *Kent*.

68 Froissart mentions his distinguished part in the battles of Crecy in 1346, Winchelsea in 1350 and Poitiers in 1356.

The great northern baronial family who, from 1377, were Earls of Northumberland. The Burgh family made little impact on national history.

70 A position (NG 657138) of some strategic importance in Buckinghamshire and site of a royal hunting-lodge.

71 Before marriage to him, she was mistress of Gloucester. She was later imprisoned on a charge of treason and magic. She died c. 1446.

72 Ralph Brooke (1553–1625) published *A Discoverie of Certaine Errours...in the much commended Britannia 1594* in 1597. This work sparked off a bitter controversy with Camden. On this, see *British Antiquity*, p. 152, and see p. 37, n. 37, *Kent*. For the foundation charter of Lewes Priory see *E.H.D.* II, 605–6. Warenne does not sign himself 'Earl of Surrey'; both William I and the future William II attest the charter.

73 Gundrada was almost certainly not William I's daughter; rather 'She was, it seems, sister to Gerbod, earl of Chester'. *E.H.D.* II, 605, n. 2, with references.

74 This is, presumably, the antiquary Jeremiah Milles (1714–84).

75 Francis Sandford in his *Genealogical History of the Kings of England* of 1677.

76 Peter le Neve (1661–1729), herald and Norfolk antiquary, published nothing, but his MS notes on Castle Acre, Norfolk, are probably intended here.

77 The inscription, attributing to her the virtues of Martha and Mary, is on a large slab of black marble of later C12. It is figured in *B. of E. Sussex*, pl. 11c.

78 He became Earl of Surrey not long before his death in 1089. *Oxf. Hist.* II, 157, n. 5. He fought at Hastings and soon after built castles at Lewes (p. 50, n. 95), Reigate (p. 11, n. 70), Allington (p. 22,

married to Edward *Burgh* descended from the Percies[69] and earls of Athol. His son Thomas was created baron *Burgh* by Henry VIII. and left a son William who had Thomas, a great patron of literature and governor of Brill,[70] whom queen Elizabeth made a knight of the Garter and Lord Lieutenant of Ireland, where he died. For Eleanor Cobham[71] of this family, wife of Humphrey duke of Gloucester, whose character was none of the best, the reader may consult the history of England.

I come now to the Earls. William Rufus* king of England, first appointed *William Warren*[s][78] governor of Surrey, with the title of earl, whose arms were chequè O and Az.[79] In his foundation charter of Lewes priory we have these words: "I have given, &c. for the soul of my lord king William who brought me into England, and for the soul of my lady Matilda the queen, mother to my wife,[80] and for that of my lord king William her son, after whose coming into England I made this charter, and who made me earl of Surrey, &c." He was succeeded[t] by his son[u] and grandson[x] of the same name: but the

*Brooke excepted to this, and asserted that the Conqueror made William Warren earl of Surrey. Camden defended himself by the express words of the foundation charter of Lewes priory. Brooke adduced the ledger book of Lewes against him, but Camden maintained his opinion without reply, and Vincent in his detection of Brooke's errors confirmed Camden.[72]

s. Who married the Conqueror's daughter.[73] Milles,[74] Sandford.[75] Le Neve MS. n.[76] See her epitaph at Lewes[77] in Sussex.

t. 1089, buried at Lewes. Dugd. I. 74.[81]   u. William, who died 1135,[82] 3 Steph. buried at Lewes. ib. 75.[83] 1138 Watson, Hist. of the family of Warren.[84]   x. William, who died 1148.[85] Dugd. Ib.

n. 02, *Kent*) and Castle Acre, Norfolk. He also founded Cluniac priories at Castle Acre and Lewes (p. 50, n. 96) and died in a siege of Pevensey Castle (p. 53, n. 17). He was buried in Lewes Priory and his leaden coffin and that of his wife were found in 1845 when a railway was being made across the site of the Priory. The coffins are now in St John the Baptist, Southover, near by.

79 This would usually be expressed as 'checky' (i.e. divided into squares as on a chessboard). 'O' is *or* (gold or yellow) and 'Az' is blue. But this William de Warenne probably had no coat of arms; they first came into use somewhat later.

80 See n. 73 above in spite of this statement.

81 William Dugdale, *Monasticon Anglicanum*, vol. I, p. 74.

82 In 1137/8. The date 1135 is a slip.

83 Ib-(idem) refers to the work cited in n. 81 above.

84 John Watson (1725–83), *Memoirs of the...Earls of Warren and Surrey*, 1776.

85 The third Earl of Surrey was a supporter of King Stephen. He died on Crusade.

last had only a daughter,[86] first married to *William*,[87] son of king Stephen, and afterwards to *Hamelin*[88] bastard son of Jeoffrey *Plantagenet* earl of Anjou; to both of whom she conveyed that title. Her first husband dying without issue,[y] Hamelin[z] had by her *William*[92] earl of Surrey, whose descendants assumed the name of *Warren*, and bore the same title. This William[a] married the eldest daughter and coheiress of William Marshall earl of Pembroke,[95] widow of Hugh *Bigod*, and had by her *John*,[b] who had by Alice daughter of Hugh *le Brun* earl of March in France, own sister to king Henry III, *William*, who died[c] before his father, and by Joan *Vere* daughter of the earl of Oxford *John*,[97] born after his father's death, last earl of this family, who was as we see on his seal[d]

y. 1159 Reg. Lewes,[89] buried at Toulouse. 1160, 3 Hen. II. Dugd. ib.76.[90]

z. He died 1202. Le Neve, ib. buried at Lewes. Reg.[91]

a. He died 1240, 24 Hen. III. buried at Lewes (Dugd. ib. 77),[93] *in medio pavimenti coram summum altare* (Reg.)[94] as was the heart of his second wife Maud, who died 1236 or 7. His natural daughter was concubine to king John.

b. He died 1304, 32 Edw. I.[96] at Kennington, and was buried at Lewes before the altar. Dugd. 78. Reg. He was a distinguished commander in Edward I's wars.

c. He was killed in a tournament at Croydon 1286, and buried before the high altar at Lewes with his wife Joan, daughter of Robert de Vere of Oxford, under a raised tomb.

d. To his settlement on Maud de Herford and her sons. Glover.[98] Dugd. I. 82 in his confirmation of Gresham advowson[99] to the monks of Thetford. Martin's[01] Hist. of Thetford, p. 185, and in his will. To a confirmation charter of John 7th earl is a seal inscribed on one side S. JOHIS DE WARENIA COMITIS SURREYA DNI DE BROMFIELD ET DE YAL:[02] on the other, S. JOHANNIS COMITIS DE WARENIA ET DE SURREYA,[03] the first out of compliment to its being an English title; the other sets the foreign[04] before it and shews the family never lost the use of it. Watson.[05]

86 Isabella (d. 1203) who at some time before 1153 married William (d. 1159), son of King Stephen, and then Hamelin (see following notes).

87 He died in 1159 while on campaign in Toulouse. The Treaty of Winchester of 1153 guaranteed to him his father's private estates and in addition, through his marriage, the estates of the Warennes. *Oxf. Hist.* III, 164–5, 202.

88 Hamelin was half-brother of Henry II and was entitled De

Warenne and Earl of Surrey by right of his wife Isabella (see n. 86 above) whom he married c. 1163. He denounced Becket as a traitor in 1164. A year before his death in 1202, he built the great castle keep at Conisbrough, Yorks.

89 The Register of Lewes Priory.

90 3 Hen. II. was 1157. See n. 81 above for 'Dugd.'.

91 See notes 88 and 90 above.

92 He was one of John's sureties for the observance of Magna Carta and

supported Louis the Dauphin in his invasion of England in 1216. *Oxf. Hist.* III, 457.

93 See n. 81 above.

94 '…in the middle of the pavement before the high altar' according to the Register (Reg.) of Lewes Priory.

95 First Earl of Pembroke and Striguil (near Usk, Mon.) who by marriage acquired the vast but scattered lands of the Clare family in England, Wales and Ireland. From almost his first appearance in history in mid-C12, he gave loyal service to successive kings and, late in life, he was regarded by the barons as a pattern of knightly virtues and of wisdom. He died in 1219. See p. 14, n. 89 above and p. 68, n. 60.

96 In 1303/4. For Kennington Palace see p. 22, n. 55.

97 He succeeded to the estates and titles in 1304, but was deprived in 1319 of most of his lands by Henry, Earl of Lancaster. He had recovered them by 1326: they finally reverted to the Crown and were granted to the Earl of Warwick. He died in 1347.

98 Robert Glover (1544–88), herald, assisted Camden in the *Britannia*. The word 'settlement' here refers to the conveyance of estates. The seal was attached to the document recording the conveyance.

99 The right of presentation to a church living, in this instance at Gresham, Norfolk.

01 'Honest Tom Martin of Palgrave' (1697–1771), antiquary. His *History of Thetford* was published by Gough in 1779.

02 'Sir John de Warenne, Earl of Surrey, Lord of Bromfield and Yale'. See p. 26, n. 06.

03 'Sir John Earl of Warenne and of Surrey'.

04 The Warenne family took its name from the château of Varenne (later Bellencombre) in the Département Seine Maritime.

05 See p. 24, n. 84.

"earl of Warren, Surrey, Strathern in Scotland, lord of Bromfield and Yale,[06] and count palatine.[e]" He dying[f] without legitimate issue 21 Edward III.[12] *Alice* his sister and heiress married to *Edmund*[13] earl of *Arundel*[g] conveyed this title to the Arundel[16] family;[h] from whence it came at length by the *Mowbrays*[23] to the *Howards*. For Thomas Mowbray married the eldest sister and coheiress of Thomas Fitz-Alan earl of Arundel and Surrey. In the mean time,[i] however, Richard II. conferred the title of duke of Surrey on *Thomas Holland* earl of Kent, who did not enjoy it long.[25] For attempting to release Richard from his imprisonment, and restore him to the throne, the design got wind too soon, and he flying was surprised by the populace at Cirencester, and beheaded. *Thomas de Beaufort*[26] who was king's chancellor, if we may believe Thomas Walsingham,[k] possessed this dignity afterwards. According to

e. *Comes Palatii*. From having regal jurisdiction in his territories. Selden's Tit. of Hon. p. 533.[07] It was some office in the king's court held by election or of antient right: as the earl of Chester carried the Curtana[08] or St. Edward's sword before Henry III. at his marriage. Math. Par. sub. a. 1236.[09]

f. 1347, 21 Edward III. on his birth day aged exactly 61, buried at Lewes under a raised tomb near the high altar. Dugd. 82.[10] Reg.[11]

g. Dugd. I. 316.[14] See a Warren pedigree Lel. Collect. I. 238.[15]

h. For Richard their son who married in the house of Lancaster (after his father was wickedly beheaded for siding with his sovereign king Edward II. by the malignant envy of the queen[17]) was both earl of Arundel and Surrey, and left both earldoms to Richard his son, who contrariwise lost his head for siding against his sovereign Richard II.[18] But Thomas his son,[19] to repair his father's dishonour, lost his life for his prince and country in France, leaving his sisters his heirs for the lands not entailed, who were married to Thomas Mowbray[20] duke of Norfolk, &c. to sir Rowland Lenthall, and sir William Beauchamp, lord of Abergavenny.[21] Holland.[22]

i. After the execution of Richard[24] earl of Arundel. Id.

k. Ypod. Neust. 571.[27]

06 Bromfield near Ludlow (Salop) and Yale, Denbighshire. The latter place-name gave name not only to the medieval lordship, but to the family of Yale, one of whom was a benefactor of the American university that bears his name.

07 John Selden (1584-1654), lawyer, Parliamentarian and orientalist. This reference is to his *Titles of Honour*, 1614.

08 The pointless sword carried before English kings at their coronation. It is also called the Sword of Edward the Confessor.

09 Matthew Paris (d. 1259), historian and monk of St Albans, of which he became chronicler from 1235. His *Chronica Majora*, a work of great historical value, is here referred to.

10 See p. 24, n. 81.

11 See p. 25, n. 94.

12 In 1347.

13 Born 1285; executed by Isabella and Mortimer in 1326 for his support of Edward II. See note *h*.

14 See p. 24, n. 81.

15 John Leland's *Collectanea* was published in 1715 by Thomas Hearne, over 150 years after Leland's death. On Leland see Appendix.

16 This Sussex title was held by the Albinis in C12 and early C13, the Fitzalans from C13 to 1580 and then by the Howards, in whose family was and is the Dukedom of Norfolk.

17 See n. 13 above.

18 This was the third Richard Fitzalan, Earl of Arundel and Surrey (1346-97), who took a principal part in the opposition to Richard II and quarrelled with John of Gaunt.

19 Thomas (1381-1415) died of dysentery after the siege of Harfleur.

20 See nn. 23 and 31 following.

21 This Sir William Beauchamp was Lord of Bergavenny, Captain of Calais and brother of Thomas, Earl of Warwick, who died in 1401.

22 Philemon Holland (1552-1637) was the first translator of the *Britannia* (1610). See Appendix.

23 Thomas Mowbray, twelfth baron Mowbray and first Duke of Norfolk (1366?-99) received part of the Arundel estates but not the title.

24 See n. 18 above. *Id.* means 'the same work, the last mentioned', i.e. Holland.

25 Born 1374, created Duke of Surrey 1397, deprived of the Dukedom in 1399 and executed 1400.

26 Sir Thomas Beaufort, Duke of Exeter, illegitimate son of John of Gaunt, was chancellor from 1410 to 1412 and died in 1427. He seems not to have held the Surrey title.

27 *Ypodigma Neustriae* (1419), concerned with events in Normandy.

that writer "in 1410 died lord Thomas Beaufort earl of Surrey."
But Walsingham[28] must take this upon himself, no such thing
appearing in the public records, only that Thomas de Beaufort
was appointed chancellor about that time.[l] But it is certain
from the records that king Henry VI. in his 29th year[30] created
John Mowbray,[31] son of John duke of Norfolk, *earl of Warren
and Surrey*.[m] Lastly, Richard III. having wickedly usurped the
crown, to attach to his interest the family of the Howards
descended from the Mowbrays, created, in the same day, John
lord *Howard*[34] duke of Norfolk, and *Thomas*[35] his son earl of
Surrey, on whose descendants this title has reflected honour,
and still continues to do so.

This county has 140 parish churches.

l. The same year. Id. 570.[29]

m. And Richard,[32] second son of king Edward IV. having married the
heir of Mowbray received all the titles due to the Mowbrays by creation
from her father. He was dispatched by Richard III. Holland.[33]

28 A monk of St Albans and
historian, he is a principal
authority for events in late C14 and
early C15.

29 See n. 24 for *Id*. The year was
1410.

30 1450/51.

31 Duke of Norfolk, hereditary
Earl Marshal and Earl of Nottingham
(1415–61).

32 He was one of the 'Princes in the
Tower'. Born 1472; created Duke
of York in 1474; married to Anne
Mowbray in 1478; and murdered
with his brother, Edward V
(1470–83) in 1483.

33 See n. 22 above.

34 First Duke of Norfolk of the
Howard line, so created in 1483, he
died in 1485 at the battle of
Bosworth.

35 He became Earl of Surrey in 1483
and Duke of Norfolk in 1514. He
had fought on the side of Edward IV
at the battle of Barnet in 1471, but
supported Richard at Bosworth in
1485. Henry VII put him in the
Tower, but he was later released and
gained the royal favour.

SELECT BIBLIOGRAPHY

References to the companion volume on Kent
are given as *Kent*

Archaeological Journal, XCII, 1935: Report of the Summer Meeting at Chichester, with Arundel, Broadwater, Amberley, Bosham, Porchester, Titchfield, Bishop's Waltham and Cowdray, 377f.; XCVII, 1940; CVII, 1950; CXIII, 1956; CXVI, 1959: Report of the Summer Meeting at Brighton, with Pevensey, Herstmonceux, Firle, Ashdown Forest, Old Shoreham, Arundel, Amberley, New Shoreham, Etchingham, Bodiam, Rye, Winchelsea and Lewes, 225f.; CXX, 1963; CXXV, 1968

Archaeology of Sussex, The, E. C. Curwen, 2nd edn, 1954

Buildings of England, The: Sussex, I. Nairn and N. Pevsner, 1965

Coastline of England and Wales, The, J. A. Steers, 1946, 304f.

Domesday Geography of South-East England, The, H. C. Darby and E. M. J. Campbell (eds.), 1962, 438f.

Glass Industry of the Weald, The, G. H. Kenyon, 1968

Knole and the Sackvilles, V. Sackville-West, 1923

Little Guides, The: Sussex, F. G. Brabant and R. F. Jessup (completely revised by R. F. Jessup), 9th edn, 1938

Medieval Archaeology, III, 1959; V, 1961; VI-VII, 1962–3; VIII, 1964; IX, 1965; X, 1966; XI, 1967; XII, 1968; XIII, 1969; XIV, 1970

New Towns of the Middle Ages, M. Beresford, 1967: Arundel, Battle, Hastings, Midhurst, Rye and New Shoreham, 491f.; Winchelsea, 14f.

Pevensey Castle (Official Guide), C. Peers, 1952

Place-Names of Sussex, The, A. Mawer and F. M. Stenton with the assistance of J. E. B. Gover, 2 vols., 1929–30

Prehistoric Sussex, E. C. Curwen, 1930

Sussex Archaeological Collections, XXI, 1869; LXII, 1922; LXXII, 1931; LXXX, 1939; LXXXVII, 1948; LXXXIX, 1950

Victoria County History, The: Sussex, especially Vol. III, 1935, on Roman Sussex

Wealden Glass, S. E. Winbolt, 1933

The General Bibliography is on page 75

SUSSEX

SOUTH of Surrey lies Sussex, a long tract of country, antiently occupied by the REGNI,[01] called by the Saxons 'Suth-sex',[02] q.d. the kingdom of the South Saxons, a name compounded of its southern situation, and the Saxons, who established here the kingdom of the Heptarchy.[03] This county is of greater length than breadth, extending along the British ocean[04] to the south, with an almost strait shore having few ports; the sea dangerous by shelves making a great swell; and the coast rocky. That part of the county which lies on the sea consists of high green hills, called *Downes*,[05] whose soil is a rich chalk and produces plenty of corn. The midland part[06] is beautifully diversified with meads, pastures, cornfields, and woods. The hithermost and north part is most pleasantly covered with woods, as was the whole country formerly, and thereby rendered inaccessible. The forest of *Andradswald*,[07] called by the Britans *Coed Andred*,[08] from the neighbouring city[09] *Anderida*, extended 120 miles in length and 30 in breadth hereabouts.[10] It was remarkable for the fate of Sigebert king of the West Saxons, who was driven from his throne, and slain in this forest by a swineherd.[11]

SUSSEX has many little rivers, but those that rise in the north edge of the county and make directly to the sea, are not fit to bear trading vessels.[12] It has several veins of iron, and many furnaces for melting it,[13] which consume great quantities of wood every year.[14] Many streams unite in one in several places, and a great deal of meadow ground is converted into lakes and

edge of the High Weald, taking in tracts of Upper Greensand, Gault Clay, Lower Greensand and Weald Clay. On the changes in the land use of the region see *Weald*, p. 233f.

07 *Andredesleage* (*Chronicle* under year 477) and *Andredesweald* (under year 1018) are more typical spellings. Both mean 'forest of Andred'. See *P.N. Sussex*, p. 1, and p. 52, n. 12.

08 *Coed* is the modern Welsh for 'trees, wood', and *Andred* is from the pre-English *Anderita*, on which see p. 52, n. 12.

09 It was not a city, but a Roman fort beside which, no doubt, there would have been a civil settlement for the camp followers. Camden believed *Anderita* to have been at Newenden, Kent, for which see p. 84, *Kent*.

10 These dimensions of the Weald are from the *Chronicle*, under 893.

11 The *Chronicle* enters this under the year 755, but owing to the error of a scribe, all the entries from 754 to 845 are dislocated and most of them, including this one, are dated two years too early. On this see *Parker Chronicle*, p. 9f. The entry for 755 reads:

In this year *Cynewulf* and the *witan* of Wessex deprived *Sigebryht* of his kingdom because of his unjust deeds, except [they left him in possession of] Hampshire; and he held this until he slew the nobleman who had stayed [loyal] to him for the longest time; and *Cynewulf* then drove him into *Andred* [the Weald], and he remained there until a herdsman stabbed him at the stream at Privett [Hants.]; whereby he avenged the nobleman *Cumbra*.

On this episode see *Oxf. Hist.* II, 208 and n. 3.

---

01 On the *Regni* (*Regnenses*), see p. 1, n. 01.

02 In the *Anglo-Saxon Chronicle* it is *Suthseaxe* or *Suthsexe*, the reference being to the people of the South Saxons and not to their territory.

03 'Heptarchy' is a term avoided by most modern historians because it is misleading. It refers to the seven kings and kingdoms of Northumbria, Mercia, East Anglia, Essex, Kent, Sussex and Wessex; but from the time of Edwin of Northumbria, who reigned from 617 to 633, three of them, Northumbria, Mercia and

Wessex, overtopped the rest. Even before that time it is difficult to be sure in some periods whether Deira, Lindsey or the Hwicce are to be counted in the seven instead, say, of Essex. But compare *History of the Anglo-Saxons*, p. 274, or *Medieval Foundations of England*, pp. 31–2.

04 The English Channel. The North Sea was called the German Ocean.

05 The South Downs.

06 'The midland part' presumably stretched from the scarp of the South Downs northward to the

12 See *Sussex Arch. Coll.* LXXII, p. 167f. and figs. 5 and 6.

13 See E. Straker, *Wealden Iron*, 1931.

14 See *Hist. Geog. Eng.*, p. 358.

29

15 Many of these old hammerponds still exist in the Weald (see e.g. *B. of E. Sussex*, pl. 2b; *Med. Eng.*, fig. 99). Some of them later provided a head of water to drive cornmills, others are ornamental waters on private estates. Ironworking in the region, especially along the Forest Ridge in East Sussex, began in the period immediately before the Roman conquest and continued during the Roman occupation, especially during C2 and C3 A.D. See *Arch. Sussex*, pp. 264, 294; and *Med. Arch.* IX, 217; XI, 318; XII, 210; XIV, 207 for sites. In the Domesday Survey of 1086, a *ferraria* is mentioned on an unspecified holding in East Grinstead and the industry is occasionally noticed in later medieval records. Its main centres were at Buxted, Burwash, Penhurst, Maresfield, Ashburnham, Hartfield and Etchingham. The primitive 'blooming' process gave way to the blast furnace in early C16, but the industry declined rapidly in early C18. Nevertheless the Ashburnham works continued in production until 1828. See e.g. *Hist. Geog. Eng.*, p. 357, and p. 58, n. 58 below. In 1574, when Camden was still a young man, there were 38 forges and 32 furnaces in Sussex. See *Med. Eng.*, pp. 235–7, and *Weald*, p. 227, for a map of iron-working sites. See also p. 3, n. 26, *Kent*.

16 Camden probably had in mind Ralph Hogge of Buxted, one of a family of ironfounders, who is said to have cast the first (English) cannon in 1543. His house, with the Hogge rebus over the door, is near Buxted church.

17 See *Wealden Glass*, and *The Glass Industry of the Weald*. The main concentration of this industry was round Chiddingfold and Alfold, Surrey, and Kirdford and Wisborough Green in West Sussex. Gough (*Additions*, p. 192) says: 'Here is not now a single glasshouse [i.e. glass works] in the county.' This was in 1789.

pools[15] to turn mills which move hammers to work iron, whose incessant noise night and day echoes all over the neighbourhood. But the iron melted here, either from the natural quality or management of the metal, is not of the same goodness, and in general [is] more brittle than the Spanish iron. It yields however no small profit to the proprietors of the mines who cast cannon[16] and other articles in it. How far it will be of public utility time must shew. Nor are glass houses wanting here; but the glass which they make, either from the quality or method of melting it, is less pure and transparent, and fit only for common use.[17]

The civil division of this county is into six parts, called by a name peculiar to it, *Rapes*.[18] These are Chichester, Arundel, Brembre,[19] Lewes, Pevensey, and Hastings; each of which, besides hundreds, has its own castle, river, and forest. But as I am not acquainted with the exact bounds of these divisions, I shall confine myself to a survey of the coast from west to east. The inner parts of the county being thick set with villages have nothing very remarkable.

On the edge of this county and Hants stands *Bosenham*, commonly called *Boseham*,[20] surrounded with woods and the

18 'Rape', in this sense, is first recorded in the Domesday of 1086 and is derived from Old English *rāp*, 'rope'. In this usage it refers 'to the fencing off of land with a rope' (*Etym. Dic.*, p. 739) and, by an extension of meaning, 'the land thus fenced off, a land-division'. *Oxf. Hist.* II, 291, 496, 617, 620, considers that the rapes were ancient Saxon provinces which, soon after the Norman Conquest, became feudal castelries, each rape being placed under the lordship of a separate baron and named from his chief local castle; but Chichester and Arundel rapes were both put under Roger, Earl of Shrewsbury. On the other hand Salzman, *Arch. Journ.* CXVI, p. 229, considers that the rapes were created after the Norman Conquest. Each 'had a harbour, a road towards London and a castle. Originally he [William I] seems to have given the whole of Sussex west of the river Adur to Earl Roger of Montgomery as the Rape of Arundel; east of the river were formed the Rapes of Lewes, Pevensey and Hastings. A few years later, probably about 1075, a new rape was made for William de Braose out of adjacent parts of Arundel and Lewes and centred upon the castle of Bramber.' See also *P.N. Sussex* I, 8f.

19 For an account of recent excavations at Bramber Castle see *Med. Arch.* XI, 285–6; XII, 178.

20 Bosham is a lovely village with a partly Saxon church built on a Roman site. See *B. of E. Sussex*, p. 110f. and pl. 10b; plan in *Arch. Journ.* XCII, 412. The place-name probably meant '*Bosa's* homestead (*hām*)'. *P.N. Sussex*, p. 58. But see J. McN. Dodgson in *Anglo-Saxon England* 2, 1973, ed. P. Clemoes, p. 25.

sea, where as Bede[a] relates, "Dicul, a Scotch monk, had a very small monastery and five or six brethren serving God in poverty."[22] This place long after became the retreat of king Harold, who from hence putting his vessel out to sea for his pleasure[b] was driven by contrary winds to the French coast, where he was seized and detained till he had confirmed by oath the kingdom of England to William the Norman after the death of Edward the Confessor, which action proved the ruin of himself and England.[24] By what an artful ambiguity that cunning word-catcher Godwin,[25] earl of Kent, father of Harold, possessed himself of this place, cheating the archbishop by ensnaring words,[c] Walter Mapes,[27] who lived not many years after, will tell you in his own words in his book de Nugis Curialium.[d] "Godwin having seen Boseham below Chichester coveted it, and accompanied with a great troop of nobles waited on the archbishop, to whom it then belonged, and in a smiling jocular manner says to him, "My lord, give me Boseam.[e]" The archbishop wondering what he meant replied, "I give you Boseam." Immediately Godwin and all his soldiers as was concerted fell at his feet, and returning him many thanks withdrew to Boseham, and violently kept possession of it, extolling the archbishop to the king for his liberality to which his own people had been witnesses; and so he quietly enjoyed it."[29] Afterwards, as we read in Testa de Nevill, an inquisition

a. Eccl. Hist. IV.13.[21]

b. *Sui colligendi causa*. One would think Camden means, *to recover his patrimony*.[23]

c. *litterarum tendiculis*.[26]

d. In MS. in the Bodleian library, Arch. B.52. and Jame's extracts from it, Ib. MS. XIV. Tan. B.B. 508.[28]

e. Alluding probably to the kiss (*basium*) given antiently in token of homage.

21 *Ecclesiastical History*, Book IV, ch. 13.

22 Fragments of a successor to Dicul's monastery are said to be built into the Old Manor House and a cottage. *B. of E. Sussex*, p. 112. It had been refounded by William Warelwast, Bishop of Exeter (1107–37).

23 Gough, *Additions*, p. 193, offers an interpretation different from the one he gives here: 'I should rather refer it to his intention of *ransoming his relations*.' On the previous page he notes that Eadmer (*Historia Novorum* I, 29) 'says he asked the king's leave to go to Normandy to fetch his brother and nephew who were kept as hostages there'. But see *Oxf. Hist.* II, 569, and *The Normans*, pp. 127–32. This visit took place in 1064.

24 See *Oxf. Hist.* II, 569, and *The Bayeux Tapestry* X, 3.

25 Godwine (d. 1053), Earl of the West Saxons, was both wealthy and powerful. He aided Edward the Confessor to succeed peacefully to the throne and Godwine's daughter became queen. He opposed Edward's pro-Norman policies and increased his influence by gaining the earldom of East Anglia for his son Harold and the earldom of parts of Mercia for his son Swegen. Outlawed with his sons in 1051, he was restored to the royal favour after displays of military strength. His treachery was exemplified by his murder of Alfred the Atheling, on which see *Two Saxon Chrons.* II, 211–15, and p. 6, n. 43.

26 Literally 'by snares of words'.

27 Walter Mapes, or Map (c. 1137–c. 1205?) was one of the most versatile authors of C12. See *Camb. Hist. Eng. Lit.* I, 177f., 188f. He may not himself have regarded this story as history.

28 Arch. B.52 is a reference to a Bodleian press number. The final section of the note refers to Tanner, *Bibliotheca Britannico-Hibernica* (an account of early C17 authors of the three kingdoms of Great Britain), p. 508, published in 1748. The second reference is probably to Richard James (1592–1638), librarian to Sir Robert Cotton, the friend of Camden, whose MSS were acquired by the Bodleian in 1676. Thomas Tanner (1674–1735), antiquary and Bishop of St Asaph, provided the additions for Wilts. to Gibson's edition of the *Britannia*. His *Notitia Monastica* (1695) are frequently cited in Gough's footnotes.

29 The manor remained in the possession of the family of Godwine until the Norman Conquest. By then its head, King Harold, was possessed of enormous wealth in lands. *Domesday Book and Beyond*, p. 208.

30 *Testa de Neville* is the former name of the *Book of Fees*, H.M.S.O., 1921–31, which 'contains returns (to the Exchequer) of inquisitions, lists of fees &c.', *Oxf. Hist.* III, 503. Jollan de Neville (d. 1246), a judge, was possibly the author of all or part of the *Testa*. See also *V.C.H., Sussex*, IV, 181f.

31 Gough presumably means the enquiry of 1279. *Oxf. Hist.* IV, 358–9.

32 The Domesday Book entry for Hertford has a valuation of the township as £7–10–0 by tale (i.e. counted coin by coin) in 1066 and £20 *arsas et pensatas*, 'assayed and weighed', in 1086. See *E.H.D.* II, 513–15, 570. These were contrasting methods of reckoning money. The 'pound sterling' implies weight, of course, for it was originally a pound, by weight, of silver. See also *English Coins*, p. 81.

33 William Marshal (d. 1219), by marriage to 'the heiress of Richard earl of Pembroke, became the possessor of the earldom and of the enormous, if scattered, estates of the family of Clare [p. 14, n. 89; p. 25, n. 95] in England, Ireland and Wales'. *Oxf. Hist.* III, 297.

34 This is a correct reconstruction of the original form of the place-name, but the earliest extant form, of C9, is *Cisseceastre*. *P.N. Sussex*, p. 10. *Caer Cei* is not in Nennius' list, p. 5, n. 53, *Kent*.

35 The greater part of the circuit of the walls survives. The Roman city of *Noviomagus Regnensium* was apparently not walled until 'some years earlier than 200' (*Brit.*, p. 250) and the bastions were added in about 370 (*Brit.*, p. 256). 'The masonry of the city wall in its present form is medieval or later, probably encasing a core of Roman work' (*Arch. Sussex*, p. 274). This rampart, with bastions, is best seen from the meadows to the south-west of the city, with a splendid view of the mass of the Cathedral. For a plan

of land [30] taken in the reign of John,[f] "king William who came to the Conquest of England, gave this to William Fitz Aucher and his heirs in fee, paying yearly to the Exchequer 40 pounds of silver, tried and weighed (*arsæ & ponderatæ*),[32] and afterwards William Marshall [33] held it by right of inheritance."

Chichester Cathedral, engraved by Wenceslaus Hollar

Chichester, in Britain *Caer Cei*, in Saxon 'Cissanceaster',[34] in Latin *Cicestria*, lies more inland in a level plain on the same bay. It is a tolerably large city, walled round,[35] built by and called after Cissa, the second Saxon prince of this province.[36] *Cissanceaster* means nothing more than the *City of Cissa*, whose father

f. Rather in that of Edward I.[31]

of the town and its walls see *Arch. Journ.* XCII, 384–5, and for an aerial view *Med. Eng.*, pp. 176–7 and fig. 71. See also *South-East England*, pp. 179–80.

36 According to the *Anglo-Saxon Chronicle*, under the year 477, 'Ælle and his three sons, Cymen, Wlencing and Cissa, came to the land of the Britons in three ships in the place called Cymenes ora and there slew many Welshmen and

drove some in flight into the forest called Andredes leag.' Cymenes ora may have been on a lost land surface (NG c. 830930) now known as the Owers (*P.N. Sussex*, p. 83). It has been estimated 'that there was an annual loss of one to three yards of land' during C19. The process of coastal erosion here has probably been continuous for several thousand years and is still going on. See *Weald*, pp. 100, 196–7, and *Coastline*, p. 304.

Ella first founded the Saxon kingdom here. It was of little note before the Norman government, and remarkable only for a monastery of St. Peter,[37] and a small nunnery.[38] But in the time of William I. as we find in the Domesday book,[g] "here were 100 *hagæ*[39] or houses, and this city was in the hands of earl Roger,[*] and there are in the same dwelling places[h] 60 houses more than there were before. It paid £.15. to the king, and 10 to the earl.[i]" When afterwards in the reign of the Conqueror it was enacted, that the episcopal sees should be transferred from little towns to places of more note,[41] it began to acquire consequence from the bishop's residence, which had before been in Selsey.[42] A few years after, bishop Ralph built a church,[43] which he had scarce finished when it was burnt down by accident.[44] By his assistance, however, and the liberality of king Henry I. it recovered itself again, and has now besides the bishop, a dean, præcentor, chancellor, treasurer, two arch-deacons, and 30 prebendaries. At the same time the city began to flourish, and would have arisen to great splendor had not the harbour been at too great distance and inconvenient. The citizens, however, are endeavouring to make it more commodious by cutting a new canal.[45] The city is of a circular form within the walls, and washed on all sides except the north by the little river *Lavant*. It has four gates[46] pointing to the four quarters of the world, from which the streets run in a strait line, and intersect each other in the centre, where stands the market-place, and where bishop Robert Read built a beautiful

Roger [de Montgomery] and there are on the same burgages 60 houses more than had been earlier (*et sunt in eisdem masuris lx domus plusque antea fuerant*), and one mill rendering 5s. It used to return £15, £10 to the king and 100s. to the earl. Now it is worth £25, and yet it returns £35. Humphrey Flamme has there one *haga* rendering 10s.

(*Domesday Geog. S.E. Eng.*, pp. 438, 465.) A very conjectural estimate of the City's population would put it between 1200 and 1500.

40 'on the same burgages', see previous note.

41 In about 1072 the East Anglian see of North Elmham, Norfolk, was removed to Thetford; in 1075 the sees of Lichfield, Selsey and Sherborne were removed to Chester, Chichester and Old Sarum (Wilts.) and later, but before 1086, that of Dorchester, Oxon., was transferred to Lincoln. *Oxf. Hist.* II, 658–9.

42 The site of the Saxon cathedral was destroyed by coastal erosion. See n. 36 above.

43 Ralph de Luffa became bishop in 1091 and enough of the new cathedral had been built for its dedication in 1108.

44 This fire was in 1114. There was a further consecration in 1184 and another greater fire in 1187, with subsequent rebuilding and re-consecration in 1199. The Cathedral now is essentially, and almost completely from some angles of view, Norman; and a very lovely building it is, in a lovely setting. For a history and description of it see *B. of E. Sussex*, pp. 128–68; for a large-scale plan *Arch. Journ.* XCII, 370.

45 The present canal basin (NG 859041) is of 1824. *B. of E. Sussex*, p. 185.

46 None survives. They were destroyed in the 'age of enlight-ment', the late C18. For an aerial view of the city and its walls see *Med. Eng.*, pp. 176–7 and pl. 71.

*de Montgomery. [See n. 48.]

g. P. 23.

h. *in iisdem mansuris*.[40]

i. Mr. Camden misread the last sentence. It paid £.15. £.10. to the king, and 100 shillings to the earl. *Reddebat* xv *lib. regi* x *lib. comiti* c *solid.* [See n. 39.]

37 Probably a major Saxon church (Old English *mynster* from Latin *monasterium* – *Elements* II, 46–7) which was perhaps incorporated into the north transept of the Cathedral.

38 There is no reliable record of a nunnery here; but see *Med. Arch.* XIII, 250, and the O.S. *Map of Monastic Britian*.

39 In fact, 232½ *hagae*. The Old English word *haga* originally meant 'hedge, enclosure', but later 'messuage, property'. *Elements* I, 221. The Domesday Book entry reads:

In Chichester city, in the time of King Edward, there were 97½ *hagae* (*c hagae ii et dimidia minus*) and 3 crofts (*croftae*) and they returned [in tax] 49s. less 1d. The city itself is now in the hand of Earl

47 This is the Market Cross of 1501 built by Bishop Storey, not Read. *B. of E. Sussex*, pp. 175–6; *Arch. Journ.* XCII, 396.

48 The mutilated motte alone remains of Roger's castle. He became Earl of Shrewsbury and Arundel after the Conquest, for which he contributed 60 ships. He founded Shrewsbury Abbey (where he finally became a monk), and he built several Welsh border castles. He died about 1093. The castle at Chichester was slighted at the end of John's reign. *Arch. Journ.* XCII, 384; and see p. 36, n. 79.

49 Near the site of the castle stands the splendid choir of the Greyfriars church, 'built soon after the Friary was refounded on this site in 1269'. *B. of E. Sussex*, p. 169. The rest of this church was probably never built. *Arch. Journ.* XCII, 395–6.

50 The palace is approached through a gatehouse of early C14. The main house was much altered in C18. The chapel is of early C13 and there are other parts of the palace from C13 to C14. For details see *B. of E. Sussex*, pp. 163–6. Almost the whole of this city, as well as the Cathedral Close, is visually delightful and worthy of much ambling.

51 The present Deanery dates from 1725.

52 Only a part of the C14 Hall of Wiccamical Prebends exists. The Vicars' Hall, of late C14, has a late C12 undercroft; the Vicars' Close was of late C15, but was much altered in C18. See *Med. Arch.* III, 224, 248–9.

53 He died in 1204 after having rebuilt much of the Cathedral. See n. 44 above.

54 The central tower and spire collapsed in 1861 and were remade in replica.

55 This painting on wooden panels is by Lambert Bernard of c. 1520, restored in C18. See *Arch. Journ.* CXIII, 108f. and pl. xiii–xix.

piazza of hewn stone.[47] The castle,[48] which was not far from the north gate, and was the residence of the earls of Arundel, who from hence wrote themselves earls of Chichester, was afterwards turned into a house of Franciscans.[49] The interval between the west and south gate is occupied by the cathedral, the bishop's palace,[50] and the houses of the dean [51] and prebendaries,[52] which were again destroyed by fire about the time of Richard I. Seffrid, second bishop of that name,[53] rebuilt the whole. It is not very large, but extremely neat, with a lofty stone spire,[54] and on one side of the south transept is curiously painted the history of the foundation of the church with figures of the kings of England, and on the other side those of all the bishops both of Selsey and Chichester,[55] at the expence of bishop Robert Shirburn,[56] who in the reign of Henry VIII. greatly beautified this church, and caused his motto to be painted about it, *Credite operibus*, and, *Dilexi decorem domus tuæ, Domine*.[57] The great tower near the west end of the church is said to have been built by Richard Riman of the stones he had prepared to build a castle on his neighbouring manor of Aplederham,[58] which he was not permitted to do.[59]

Selsey, Saxon 'Seals-ey',[60] which Bede translates the habitation of seals or sea calves, who always frequent islands and coasts in breeding time,[61] lies a little lower. "A place," says Bede,[k] "surrounded by the sea except to the west, on which is the entrance about a stone's throw over." It was reckoned to

k. Hist. Eccl. IV.13.

56 Sherborne (1440?–1536) had been Dean of St Paul's and forged a papal bull appointing himself as Bishop of St David's. He went to Chichester in 1508.

57 'Trust in deeds' (rather than in words) and 'I have delighted in adorning Thy house, O Lord'.

58 Appledram (NG 840030).

59 See 'The House of William Ryman', *Sussex Arch. Coll.* LXXX, 148f. There is no truth in the tradition reported by Camden, but an interesting manor-house of C15 survives. *B. of E. Sussex*, pp. 85–6.

60 This is an untypical spelling that Camden has chosen and he has

mistranslated Bede's explanation of the name. It is from OE *seolh*, 'a seal', and *ēg*, 'island', which Bede said 'was called in Latin "the island of the marine calf"' (*insula vituli marini*)', there being no word for 'seal' in Latin. Selsey was an island until early C19. *P.N. Sussex*, pp. 82–3.

61 They have not bred, in recent times at any rate, on the South Coast. The fact that the form of the place-name is 'seal's' (genitive singular) island, possibly indicates a naming of the place from a single specimen, far from its haunts and so significant enough to prompt such a naming.

contain 87 families [62] when Edilwalch [63] king of this province gave it to the exiled bishop of York Wilfrid, [64] who first preached Christianity to the people here, and "saved," as he expresses it, "250 slaves, not only by baptism from the bondage of the devil, but rescued them from the yoke of human bondage by restoring them to their liberty." Afterwards king Ceadwalla [65] who defeated Edilwalch founded a monastery here, and placed in it the episcopal see, which was transferred by Stigand the 22d bishop to Chichester, [66] where it now flourishes, and acknowledges Cedwalla [67] for its founder. In this island is the scite of the old city [68] where those bishops sat, covered by the sea when the tide is in, but clear and visible when at low water.

The shore gives passage to a river which runs from *St. Leonard's forest* [69] first by *Amberley*, where William [70] Read bishop of Chichester t. Edward III. built a castle [71] for his

67 Cædwalla may have made grants of land to Wilfrid in the area just outside the Selsey peninsula, in the modern parishes of Pagham, Bognor, Bersted and Mundham, but there is much doubt about the genuineness of the charter recording the grant (no. 230 in *A.S. Charters*) and of another (no. 232) which sets out a grant of land mainly to the west and north of the block mentioned above. Moreover, the South Saxon kings Nunna, Nothelm and Æthelberht made grants of land in C8 that partly coincide with what was supposed to have been given by Cædwalla in late C7; and the charters of Nunna and Nothelm are considered genuine. A grant by the same Æthelberht to Wilfrid of land at Chichester is recorded in another charter which is almost certainly spurious. For detailed references see *A.S. Charters*, pp. 82–3, 128, 129, nos. 42, 45, 47, 230 and 232. Cædwalla as the founder of the monastery at Selsey and, by transference, of Chichester, is therefore somewhat improbable, though there is just the possibility that the later grants were mere confirmations, or re-grantings, of what the West Saxon king had given earlier.

68 The site has been lost through erosion. See p. 32, n. 36.

69 The sources of the river Arun and Ouse, running south, and the Mole, running north, are situated in this region of higher ground (NG 230320 etc.).

70 He was consecrated bishop in 1369 and died in 1385.

71 Amberley Castle is most impressive when seen from across the Brooks (water-meadows). It was built in 1377, taking in a much older manor-house of the bishops of Chichester. *Sussex Arch. Coll.* LXII, 30f., and *B. of E. Sussex*, pp. 80–82, pl. 31a; plan in *Arch. Journ.* XCII, 410. The village, too, is most pleasing to the eye.

62 Bede (*H.E.* IV, 13) says 87 hides. A hide was a notional area of land adequate to support a free peasant and his household. *Oxf. Hist.* II, 275–6.

63 Æthelwalh, King of the South Saxons, was baptized shortly before 675. Wulfhere, King of Mercia, his godfather at the font, conquered the Isle of Wight and some of the opposite mainland and gave it to Æthelwalh. It had been West Saxon (originally Jutish) territory. Cædwalla, King of Wessex, harried Sussex (n. 65 below), killed Æthelwalh and regained the lost West Saxon territory.

64 Wilfrid had been an advocate of Roman usages in the Church, as against Celtic, and he pressed them at the Synod of *Streoneshalh* (probably Whitby) in 663. In the following year he was made bishop in Northumbria, with his see at Ripon; and in 669 was translated to the bishopric of York; but falling foul of Ecgfrith, King of Northumbria, he was expelled from there in 677 and made his way to Rome to appeal to the Pope. Although his

appeal was successful, he was exiled again from Northumbria and eventually found refuge in Sussex. Before his death in 709 he was in conflict with Ecgfrith's successor as well as with the archbishop of Canterbury. For a summary of his life, with references, see Plummer's *Bede* II, 316f.

65 King of Wessex. He 'began to strive for the kingdom' in 685; 'devastated Kent and Wight' in 686 and Kent again in 687; and departed for Rome, baptism and death in 688, according to the *Anglo-Saxon Chronicle*, MS 'A'. It was during a period of exile from Wessex that Cædwalla devastated Sussex and killed its king (n. 63 above). After seizing the throne of Wessex, he killed *Berthun*, an ealdorman, one of the two who had taken over the kingdom of Sussex. *H.E.* IV, 15, and see n. 67 below.

66 He died in 1086 (correctly 1087) according to the *Chronicle*. He is not to be confused with his near contemporary and namesake, the usurping Archbishop of Canterbury, who died in 1072.

72 The earliest recorded instance of this place-name now known is *Harundel(le)* in Domesday (1086). Its derivation is most probably from OE *hār-hūne-dell*, 'horehound valley'. *P.N. Sussex*, pp. 136–7. This plant, commonly called '(White) Horehound', *Marrubium vulgare*, is only locally common and is listed by Gough (p. 208) as occurring 'on rubbish and on the sides of ways; about *Brighthelmstone*' (i.e. Brighton). He was no doubt unaware of the derivation of the name Arundel. The plant was valued medicinally (*British Plants and their Uses*, p. 101): perhaps this was the reason for its giving name to a place.

73 Gough, p. 196, rightly points out that Camden misread the *Crundellan* of Alfred's Will. The bequest was to *Æthelhelm* and the place was Crondall, Hants. See *E.H.D.* I, 494.

74 The erroneous siting of *Portus Adurni* at the mouth of the river Adur was probably first made by Michael Drayton in his *Polyolbion* of 1622. The river gained its modern name, Adur, as a result of this mistake. *Portus Adurni* has been identified with Walton Castle, Suffolk, now destroyed by the sea (*Arch. Journ.* XCVII, 138, n. 2 and references there), and with Porchester, Hants. (e.g. O.S. *Map of Roman Britain* and pp. 27, 41 of text, both with a query mark). For earlier names of the river Adur see *P.N. Sussex*, p. 3 and n. 78 below.

75 This refers to the popular verse romance *Sir Bevis of Hamtoun* (Southampton), of early C14. W. P. Ker said of it: 'Perhaps *Sir Beves* is the best example of the ordinary popular tale, the medieval book of chivalry with all the right things in it.' Drayton retold the tale in his *Polyolbion*, written between 1613 and 1622, but Camden must have known it from the earlier version. See *Camb. Hist. Eng. Lit.* I, 305. Bevis's name was remembered in the naming of a long barrow

successors: and afterwards by *Arundell*[72] on the side of a hill; a place greater in name than reality, yet not very old; for I have not met with its name before the time of Alfred, who left it by will to Athelm his brother's son;[73] unless we should suppose *Portus Adurni*[74] a corrupt transposition for *Portus Arundi*. Its name is derived not from *Arundell*[75] the fabulous horse of Beavis,[75] nor from *Charud* a promontory of the Cimbrian Chersonesus[76] as Goropius Becanus[77] dreamed, but from the valley in which it lies on the river *Arun*, if indeed *Arun* be the name of that river as some assert,[78] who from thence call it in Latin *Aruntina vallis*. All its renown is derived from the castle which flourished in the Saxon times,[79] and was rebuilt immediately after the arrival of the Normans by Roger de Montgomery,[80] thence called earl of Arundel. It is large and extremely well fortified.[81] But his son Robert de Belesme who succeeded his brother Hugh, being attainted by Henry I.

destroyed in recent times (at NG 693065), known as Bevis's Grave.

76 The Cimbrian Chersonesus was a peninsula inhabited in early times by the Cimbri, a Celtic tribe. Charud is derived from the name of another tribe, the Charoudes or Harudes, who lived in the eastern part of the peninsula. *Origin of the English Nation*, p. 182. Today the peninsula has Denmark in the northern and middle parts, Schleswig in the southern.

77 An elusive figure, not worthy of pursuit.

78 The river-name Arun is a back-formation from the place-name Arundel. Leland (*L.T.S.* IV, 93) knew it (c. 1550) as the 'Arundel streame', but by 1577 it is recorded as Arun(-us), Aron. Until C13 at least it was called *Tar(r)ente*, which is derived from the British river-name *Trisantona*, as are the Trent of the Midlands and Glos. and the Tarrant of Dorset. See *P.N. Sussex*, pp. 3–4; *Lang. & Hist.*, p. 503.

79 There is no evidence for a pre-Norman stronghold at Arundel itself, but across the river at Burpham is the earthwork of a

Saxon *burh* (NG 038085). It is a 'fine promontory fort...built...by the Saxons as a fortress to guard the valley of the Arun, and so was in a sense the precursor of Arundel Castle'. *Prehistoric Sussex*, p. 73. For other Saxon *burhs* in Sussex see p. 51, n. 01, and for King Alfred's system of defences against the Danes, of which these formed a part, see *Oxf. Hist.* II, 261–3. For a sketch-plan of the Burpham fort, see *Earthwork of England*, fig. 212, p. 642.

80 See p. 34, n. 48 above.

81 The castle is an impressive pile from a distance, but it is mostly modern, 'the pretty complete building of an imitation castle'. Beginning with a motte and two baileys in late C11, it had a shell-keep added by Henry II on the top of the motte and he in late C12 and Edward I in late C13 further developed the defences and living quarters. It was held for the king for 17 days in 1643 and then slighted by Waller. Even worse was the rebuilding of 1890–1903. See *B. of E. Sussex*, pp. 91–3, and C. V. Wedgwood, *The King's War*, 1958, p. 269.

forfeited this and his other honors.[82] For having traiterously stirred up a war against the king, he made this castle the seat of it, and added considerable works to it, but with the success that usually attends rebels. For the king's forces surrounding it on every side at last made themselves masters of it. Robert being attainted and banished, the king gave this castle and his other estates in dower to his second queen Adeliza,[83] daughter of Godfrey *Barbutus* of Lovain, duke of Lorrain and Brabant.[84] In her praise one of our countrymen wrote these lines, which do not breath the spirit of that illiterate age:[1]

> *Anglorum regina, tuos, Adeliza, decores*
>   *Ipsa referre parans Musa stupore riget:*
> *Quid diadema tibi pulcherrima? Quid tibi gemma?*
>   *Pallet gemma tibi, nec diadema nitet.*
> *Deme tibi cultus, cultum natura ministrat.*
>   *Non exornari* forma beata potest.*
> *Ornamenta cave, nec quicquam luminis inde*
>   *Accipis; illa micant lumine clara tuo.*
> *Non puduit modicas de magnis dicere laudes,*
>   *Nec pudeat dominam te, precor, esse meam.*

> When Adeliza's beauties grace my song,
> Amazement stops the willing muse's tongue.
> Can crowns or jewels lustre give to you?
> How poor a crown, how pale all jewels shew!
> Nature supplies Attire's superfluous toil;
> A beauteous person cannot want a foil.
> To you no beauty ornaments can give;
> From you themselves a lustre must receive.
> Yet while your praise my humble verse makes known,
> Disdain not, mighty queen, my verse to own.

On the king's death she married William de *Albini*,†[m][89] who siding with the empress Maud against king Stephen, and defending this castle against him, had the title of earl of Arundel conferred on him in reward of his services by the empress Maud "Lady of England," which was her usual style. Her son king Henry II. gave the whole *rape* of *Arundel* to this

l. See Hen. Huntingd. VII. p. 218. b.[85]
* Some copies read *meliorari*.[86]
† *D'Albineto, D'Albineio, D'Albiniaco*.[87]
  m. Dugd.[88] I. 118. where see his bold and free speech to the Pope about Becket, and that of the widow of Hugh 5th earl to Henry III. on his injustice.

82 He became Earl of Shrewsbury in 1098. He 'had played a leading part, wholly unscrupulously, in almost every trouble that had arisen during the previous reign'. He was finally imprisoned from 1112 until his death. The royal seizure of his castles of Arundel, Tickhill, Bridgnorth and Shrewsbury (he surrendered in the last of these) was in 1102. *Oxf. Hist.* III, 117–18.

83 A descendant of Charlemagne, she married Henry I in 1121. She is said to have patronized literature. She died in 1151.

84 On the policy that led to this marriage and its lasting consequences, see *Oxf. Hist.* III, 126–7 and n. 3.

85 On Henry of Huntingdon see p. 22, n. 59.

86 '…(cannot be) improved'.

87 Later (D')Aubeney. The form *D'Albineio* is probably a scribal error for *D'Albineto*.

88 Dugdale, *Monasticon Anglicanum*, vol. I. Sir William Dugdale (1605–86), one of the great antiquaries of C17, held appointments in the College of Arms. He became Garter King of Arms and a Knight in 1677. Among his published works are *Monasticon Anglicanum* (3 vols., 1655, 1661, 1673), an account of English monasteries, compiled in collaboration with Roger Dodsworth; the *Antiquities of Warwickshire*, 1656; a *History of St Paul's Cathedral*, 1658; and the *Baronage of England*, 1675–6.

89 His first wife was daughter of Roger Bigod, Earl of Norfolk. When the Empress Matilda ('Maud' in Camden) landed in England in September, 1138, she found refuge at Arundel with Albini and Adeliza. *Oxf. Hist.* III, 138. He died in 1176.

90 This was the force required by the king, properly trained and equipped, for service in his wars. See *Oxf. Hist.* II, 671–4; III, 12f.

91 *Cartae Antiquae*, 'Ancient Charters'. See *Oxf. Hist.* III, 491.

92 I.e. 'every third penny', 'a third part of the profits of justice done in the shire court'. *Oxf. Hist.* II, 539. In 1130 this, for the earldom of Arundel (or Sussex), was 20 marks. *Oxf. Hist.* III, 157, n. 4. A mark was 13s. 4d., nominally two thirds of a pound weight of silver.

93 He died in 1243. On the family of Albini see p. 67.

94 See p. 42, n. 13.

95 1267–1302.

96 'The lands which formed a lord's endowment were known collectively as his honour.' *Oxf. Hist.* II, 619.

97 Demesne consisted of the lands not granted to sub-tenants, but kept in the lord's own hands and farmed to maintain his own household. *Oxf. Hist.* II, 474.

98 John VI, Earl of Arundel (1408–35), was recognized as Earl in 1433. By an Act of Parliament of 1627 the castle was annexed, with much else, to the earldom.

99 He was the third duke, hereditary Earl Marshal of England and fifth Earl of Nottingham. He succeeded to the Dukedom in 1432.

01 The Rolls of Parliament for the 11th year of the reign of Henry VI, i.e. 1432/33. On the Rolls see *Oxf. Hist.* IV, 346f.; V, 182, 536–7.

02 The 11th Earl was William (d. 1544); Henry was the 12th (d. 1580). Camden (1551–1623) was a contemporary of Henry and of Philip Howard, Henry's successor in the earldom. See next note.

03 Philip (1557–95) was the eldest son of Thomas Howard III, 4th

William "to hold of him by 84 knights fees and a half."[90] King Richard I. gave his son William in words to this effect,‡ "the castle of Arundell with the whole honor of Arundell and the third penny[92] of the pleas of Sussex, by which he is earl." The male line ending with the fifth earl of this surname, one[n] of the sisters and heiresses of Hugh the fifth earl[93] married John *Fitz Alan* lord of *Clun*,[94] whose great grandson Richard[o][95] "being seized of the castle, honor,[96] and demesne[97] of Arundel in demesne as in fee, and by reason of his possession of the said castle, honor, and demesne without any other reason or creation was earl of Arundel, and peaceably enjoyed the name, rank, and style of earl of Arundel, &c." as appears from the sentence given in parliament for John Fitz Alan,[98] who claimed the castle and title of Arundel against "John Mowbray duke of Norfolk,[99] right heir by the mother's side in the nearest degree." Hence it appears that "the name, style, and rank of earl is annexed to the castle, honor, and demesne of Arundel," as may be seen in the Parliament Rolls 27 Henry VI.* whence I have exactly copied this account. Of these Fitz Alans the 11th earl[p] lived in my time, and dying without male issue was succeeded by his daughter's son Philip Howard,[03] who not knowing how to put up with reflections and difficulties fell into a snare by the contrivance of those who envied him, and ended his days after having been brought into the utmost danger. His son Thomas,[04] a most honourable youth, was by king James completely restored by act of parliament to his father's honours, and discovers an eager pursuit after virtue and glory worthy his rank, and which by the affability united with it reflects great lustre on him.

Arundel has nothing remarkable[05] besides its castle and

‡ Cart. Ant. 10. m. 39.[91]

n. Isabel. Dugd. I. 121. [See p. 37, n. 88.]

o. Dugd. I. 315. [See p. 37, n. 88.]

* Parl. 11 H. VI.[01]

p. Henry.[02]

Duke of Norfolk, and in 1576 had the courtesy title of Earl of Surrey conferred on him. He became a Catholic in 1584 and was condemned to death in 1589 on the charge of having Mass said for the success of the Armada. He was not executed, but died in the Tower in 1595.

04 Thomas (1585–1646) was restored to the titles in 1604 and became a protestant in 1615. He was a great art collector. In exile from 1642, he remained loyal to Charles I.

05 In spite of harm in C19 and an excess of mock antiquity, the place

earls;[06] for as to the college[07] founded there by them since its revenues have been taken away it is fallen into decay. In the church, however, are some monuments of earls,[08] of which the most beautiful is that alabaster one in the middle of the choir, under which are buried earl Thomas and his wife Beatrix, daughter of John king of Portugal.[09] Nor can I omit the following inscription in fair gold letters in honour of Henry Fitz Alan the last earl of this family.[10]

VIRTUTI ET HONORI SACRUM

Magnanimus Heros, cujus hic cernitur effigies, cujusque hic subter sita sunt ossa, hujus territorii comes fuit: Sui generis ab Alani filio cognominatus, a Malatraverso, Clunensi, & Oswaldestrensi honoribus eximiis Dominus insuper ac baro nuncupatus: Garteriani ordinis Equestris sane nobilissimi sodalis dum vixit antiquissimus: Arundeliæ comitis Guilielmi filius unicus & successor, omniumque virtutum particeps: qui Henrico octavo, Edwardo VI, Mariæ & Elizabethæ Angliæ regibus a secretis consiliis, villæ quoque Calesiæ præfecturam gessit, & cum Henricus rex Boloniam in Morinis obsidione cinxerat exercitus sui Marescallus primarius, deinde regis fuit camerarius; ejusque filio Edwardo dum coronaretur marescalli regni officiumgerebat, eiq;[11] sicut antea patri, camerarius factus. Regnante vero Maria regina coronationis solemni tempore summus constituitur constabularius, domusque regiæ postmodum præfectus, ac consilii præses, sicut & Elizabethæ reginæ, cujus similiter hospitii Senescallus fuit.

Ita vir iste, genere clarus, publicis bene functis magistratibus clarior, domi ac foris clarissimus: honore florens, labore fractus, ætate confectus, postquam ætatis suæ annum 68 attigisset, Londini 25 die Februarii anno nostræ salutis a Christo MDLXXIX pie et suaviter in Domino obdormivit.

Joannes Lumley, baro de Lumley, gener pientissimus, supremæ voluntatis suæ vindex, socero suavissimo & patrono optimo magnificentissime funerato, non memoriæ, quam immortalem sibi multifariis virtutibus comparavit, sed corporis mortalis ergo, in spem fœlicis resurrectionis reconditi, hanc illi ex propriis armaturis statuam equestrem pro munere extremo, uberibus cum lachrymis devotissimè consecravit.

i.e.

SACRED TO VIRTUE AND HONOUR

The illustrious hero, whose figure you see here, and whose bones rest here below, was earl of this place. He derived his descent and name from Fitz Alan, his honours from Maltravers,[12] lord and

is pleasing enough to be worth lingering in. In Gough's time the town had much trade, and shipbuilding was carried on. *Additions*, p. 197. On the origin of the town see *New Towns*, p. 492; on its present state, *B. of E. Sussex*, pp. 86–95 and pl. 57, 58.

06 Beside the river, close to the bridge, are the ruins of the Maison Dieu Hospital founded in 1397. For a recent excavation of the site see *Med. Arch.* x, 181.

07 In the church of St Nicholas, the Lady Chapel and Fitzalan Chapel and, near it, parts of the c19 rebuilding of the Priory, are remnants of the college founded in 1380. *B. of E. Sussex*, pp. 86, 90. Plan of the church in *Arch. Journ.* XCII, 402. See also G. H. Cook, *Medieval Chantries and Chantry Chapels*, 1963 edn, p. 185f.

08 These monuments are of the 5th (d. 1415), 6th (d. 1421), 7th (d. 1435), 9th (d. 1487), 10th (d. 1524), 11th (d. 1544) and 12th (d. 1580) earls. See *B. of E. Sussex*, pp. 88–9 and pl. 35a. There is a monument to a Fitzalan of c14 in Chichester Cathedral, north aisle. Ibid., p. 154. The original Stansted House was theirs, and what remains of it forms part of the chapel. Ibid., p. 336.

09 Thomas (1381–1415) was the fifth Earl of Arundel.

10 Henry (1511?–80) fell from Queen Elizabeth's favour for there was more than a suspicion that as a Catholic he was involved in plots against her.

11 A contraction of 'eique', in Gibson's edition of 1695

12 Camden, in speaking of Wickhampton (i.e. Witchampton), Dorset, notes that it was 'formerly the estate of the barons Maltravers, the last of whom t. E.III. left only two daughters, one married to John Arundel grandfather of John earl of Arundel, who left to his family the title of baron Maltravers (Gough, p. 46). Langton and Worth Matravers are in the Isle of Purbeck.

REFERENCES to the HUNDREDS.

1 Dumford	21 Poynings	41 Alciston
2 Eastburne	22 Fishersgate	42 Flexborough
3 Westburne	23 Burbeech	43 Longbridge
4 Bosham	24 Tipnoake	44 Willingdon
5 Manhood	25 Windham	45 East Bourne
6 Box & Stockbridge	26 Dean	46 Dill
7 Liberty of Lodsworth	27 Preston	47 Pevensey Liberty
8 Rotherbridge	28 Whalesbone	48 Foxearle
9 Westeaswright	29 Youusmere	49 Hauxborough
10 Easteaswright	30 Hollingstrough	50 Loxfield Baker
11 Bury	31 Swanborough	51 Shoyswell
12 Avisford	32 Barcomb	52 Henhurst
13 Aldweek	33 Ringmer	53 Netherfield
14 Poling	34 Rushmonden	54 Nenfield
15 Brightford	35 East Grinstead	55 Bexhill
16 Stenning	36 Hartfield	56 Baldsloe
17 West Grinstead	37 Rotherfield	57 Battle
18 Shinglecrofs	38 Loxfield	58 Staple
19 Buttinghill	39 Shiplake	59 Goldspur
20 Street	40 Totnore	60 Gostrow 61 Guesling

A NEW MAP of SUSSEX, from the best AUTHORITIES.

Published by John Stockdale Piccadilly 26th March 1805.

Engraved by J. Cary.

Statute Miles 69½ to a Degree of Latitude

13 John Fitz Alan (1223–67) was Lord of Oswestry, Clun and Arundel.

14 He became a Knight of the Garter in 1544.

15 He resigned this post in 1564, some five years after Elizabeth's accession.

16 The now accepted year of his death, 1580, is the result of the change in 1751 from the Julian Calendar to the Gregorian Calendar. This, among other readjustments to the reckoning, moved back the beginning of the year from 25 March to 1 January. See *Methods of Chronology*, pp. 5–6.

17 Lumley (1534?–1609), like his father-in-law, was implicated in the Ridolfi Plot (J. E. Neale, *Queen Elizabeth*, 1934, p. 181f.) and imprisoned from 1569 to 1573. Camden would have known him as a fellow Antiquary of the Society founded by Dr John Parker (d. 1592) and refounded by Camden's friend Sir Robert Cotton in 1614. The Lumleys were at one time at Stansted Park, Sussex. The Lumley who died in 1609 has a monument at Cheam, Surrey, in the family chapel, for which see *B. of E. Surrey*, p. 123.

18 The (Western) Rother (see p. 65, n. 18) was originally called the Shire. 'The modern name is a late back-formation from Rotherbridge.' *P.N. Sussex*, pp. 7, xliv.

19 The fine ruins of this great house (Cowdray) 'are an absolutely consistent epitome of Tudor architecture at its plainest . . .'. *B. of E. Sussex*, p. 195. It 'took sixty years to build, under three owners', beginning after 1492. It was burnt out in 1793. Plan in *Arch. Journ.* XCII, 420; and pl. 36b in *B. of E. Sussex*.

baron Clun and Oswaldestre,[13] oldest companion of the most noble order of the garter, only son and successor to William earl of Arundel, and heir to all his virtues. He was privy counsellor to Henry VIII. Edward VI. queen Mary, and queen Elizabeth, and governor of Calais;[14] and when king Henry besieged Bologne in Picardy he was chief marshall of the army, and afterwards lord chamberlain. At the coronation of his son Edward he held the office of Marshall of England, and was chamberlain to this king as he had before been to his father. At the accession of queen Mary, he was appointed high constable for her coronation, and afterwards steward of her household, and president of the council, as also to queen Elizabeth, to whom he was also steward of the household.[15]

Thus this nobleman, illustrious by birth, more so by his discharge of his several public characters, and most illustrious both at home and abroad, loaded with honours, worn out with toil, in a good old age having reached his 68th year, devoutly and sweetly slept in the Lord at London Feb. 25, A.D. 1579.[16]

John Lumley lord Lumley,[17] his dutiful son-in-law, executor of his last will, having buried his beloved father-in-law and most excellent patron, erected at his own expence and with many tears, this statue in the habit of his order, as the last expression of regard, not to his memory, which his own many virtues render immortal, but out of respect to his mortal part here lodged in hope of a blessed resurrection.

The river which runs by Arundel rises in the north part of the county, and in its course is increased by several small streams. Of these the principal[18] is that which passes by *Cowdrey*,[19] the

Cowdray House, engraved by W. Angus after S. Bevan, 1806.

beautiful house of viscount *Montacute*,[20] and, on the other side *Midherst*,[21] which boasts the *Bohuns*[22] for its lords, who bear, Or, a cross, Az.[23] and flourished from Ingelric de Bohun[24] under Henry I. to the reign of Henry VII. who bestowed a daughter and heiress of John Bohun[25] in marriage on sir David *Owen*,[26] knight, natural son of Owen Tudor,[27] with a fine estate. These Bohuns, to mention it by the bye for the antiquity of the term, were sometime the kings *Spigurnells*,[q] or sealers of briefs by inheritance,[29] which office, together with that of Serjeant of the chapel royal, John de Bohun, son of Franco, resigned to Edward I. as I read in an old charter drawn on purpose.

Next to this we come to *Petworth*,[30] which, with its lands, William de Albini[31] earl of Arundel, gave to Joscelin de Lovain,

q. Du Cange in v. derives it from the Saxon 'Sparran' to *fasten* or *seal up*. It is also called *Espicurnantia*. Somner in v. and Kennett Gloss. to Paroch. Ant.[28]

Spigurnell was Warden of the Cinq Ports in 1370. *Lamb.*, p. 115.

30 For Petworth see the enthusiastic description, almost house by house, in *B. of E. Sussex*, p. 297f. Among Leland's very sparse notes on Sussex he says of Petworth (*L.T.S.* IV, 92):

The market towne of Petteworth yn the Wald of Southsax is right welle encreasid sins the yerles of Northumbreland usid litle to ly there. For now the men there make good clothe. The parsone of the toune hath muche pryvilege there, and concerning certen tenauntes that he hath there kepith his courte and leete [court of record]. One parson Acon buildid the spire of the faire steple there in the toune, and also made the fayre bridge of stone caullid Rotherbridge scant a mile from Peteworth apon the water that cummith doune from Cowdrey. Parson Edmundes of late dayes perceyving the great lak of water at Petworth caussid chiefly a great spring, the hedde wherof is about a mile from the toune, to be brought in lede to Petworth, parte of the water cumming to the maner place, part to the personage, the residew to ii. or iii. places yn the streate of the toune. In the chyrche of Petworth ly buried sum of Percy's childern, but none of the lordes. Ther lyith one Syr William Redmille a knight that dwellid, as I hard, in a log [lodge] of the great parke there. Ther lyith also one or ii. [of] the Scropes: and as I harde there be buried summe of the Scropes at Bosgrove Priory by (Halna)cre a late the Lord Delawar house. Ther be buried also yn Petworth Chyrch certein of the Dautereis, whose names in Latine were (there) wryten *de alta ripa* [of high bank]. The chefest house of these Dautereis is in Petworth paroche caullid the More, half a mile from Petworth toune. There is a nother house longing to them in Petworth by the chirch. About a mile lower then Rother Bridge apon the hither ripe [bank] appere *vestigia* [traces] and a mote of an auncient manor place caullid Baienet, wher, as I lernid, ons [once] Dikes, a gentilman of fair landes, sumtime lay. On the farther side of the ripe is a waren of conys [rabbits] adjacent to it.

20 See p. 58, n. 55.

21 Now Midhurst, a beautiful country town. On its origin see *New Towns*, p. 494.

22 The Bohuns were especially powerful in C13 and C14, Henry de Bohun (1176–1220) being created Earl of Hereford in 1199. His son Humphrey (d. 1274) added the Earldom of Essex to the family honours. A later Humphrey (1276–1322) married a daughter of Edward I, and William (d. 1360) was made Earl of Northampton in 1337. Yet another Humphrey (d. 1373) held the three earldoms, but having no son, his lands passed with his sisters to Thomas of Woodstock, Duke of Gloucester, and to the future Henry IV.

23 A blue (azure) cross (in shape like that of St George) on a yellow (or) background.

24 See n. 22 above.

25 He is said to have founded the nunnery of Easebourne, for which see *B. of E. Sussex*, pp. 212–13.

26 His tomb and effigy, originally at Midhurst, are now in Easebourne

church, just outside the gates of Cowdray Park. He died in 1535. The church is a nasty C19 restoration.

27 Owen was beheaded after the battle of Mortimer's Cross in 1461. He was Henry VII's grandfather.

28 These references are to: (a) W. Somner's *Dictionarium Saxonico-Latino-Anglicum* of 1659. Somner was an enthusiastic antiquary who concentrated his studies on Kent. See p. 7, n. 65, *Kent*. (b) White Kennett (1660–1718), Bishop of Peterborough, antiquary and topographer. In full the reference would read: 'See under the word [in v.] Spigurnell in the Glossary to *Parochial Antiquities attempted in the history of Ambrosden, Burcester etc.*' (new edition in 1818).

29 The personal name Spick(er)nell is said to have meant 'sealer of the king's writs in Chancery'. *Surnames*, p. 265. It is ultimately to be derived from medieval Latin *spigurnella*, the aromatic root of *Meum athamanticum*, 'spignel', which was gathered as a vegetable by the Highlanders. *British Plants*, p. 97. A Sir Ralph

31 See Camden's text, p. 37 above. Camden is in error here. Petworth

43

was bequeathed to Adeliza by Henry I and she gave it to her brother Joscelyn who, marrying Agnes de Percy, took her name.

32 Adeliza of Louvain (d. 1151) married Henry I in 1121, and on his death in 1135, she probably retired to Arundel. See p. 37, n. 83 and 89.

33 The Petworth House that Camden knew had been built by the eighth Earl of Northumberland in the 1570s and 1580s, replacing an early C14 building of which only the chapel and some walls in the cellars survive. The existing house was the work of the sixth Duke of Somerset, begun in 1688 after he had married the Percy heiress Elizabeth. See *B. of E. Sussex*, p. 301f. and pl. 42c, 43b; *Oxf. Hist.* III, 126 and n. 3 on the Brabanter.

34 'Joceline married Agnes, heir of William Perci, who assuming his wife's name, became the progenitor of the great family of Percy.' *Arch. Journ.* XCII, 399.

35 Neither (West) Tarring nor Offington appears on the modern One-Inch map. Both have been overwhelmed by the tasteless sprawl of Worthing.

36 This Baron de la Warr (1519?–95) was the one contemporary with Camden.

37 This is Broadhempston, south Devon. The arms of the Cantelupe family occur with those of de la Warr on the tomb of the Lord de la Warr, who died in 1526, in the north side of the chancel of Broadwater church, and quartered with the de la Warr arms on the tomb of the Lord de la Warr who died in 1554, in the south transept of the same church. *Sussex Arch. Coll.* LXII, 223–4; *B. of E. Sussex*, pp. 391–2. There is also a tomb of a Lord de la Warr (d. 1526) in Boxgrove Priory. *B. of E. Sussex*, p. 117 and pl. 35b. The ruins of C13, C14 and C16 at Halnaker represent the residence of this family in earlier days. *B. of E.*

a Brabanter, brother to queen Adeliza,[32] and younger son of Godfrey duke of Brabant,[33] a descendant of Charlemagne, when he married his only daughter Agnes heiress of the Percies. From that time the posterity of that Josceline held it, having assumed the name of Percy[34] as will be elsewhere observed. It is an antient and illustrious family descended from Charlemagne, with less interruption than that pedigree so much boasted of by the dukes of Lorrain and Guise. This Josceline, as I find in his donation charter, uses this title, "Josceline de Lovain, brother to queen Adeliza, Castellan of Arundel."

In a recess of the shore from the mouth of the Arun, near *Tering*, stands *Offingtons*,[35] the seat of William *West* lord *Delaware*.[36] This family of the Wests is noble and antient, increased by marriage with the heirs of *Cantelupe* of *Hempston*,[37] and *Fitz Reginald* son of Herbert; and by the heir of lord *Delaware* acquired the title of baron.[r] Near it is a military fortification surrounded with a rude bank of earth,[38] where the inhabitants believe Cæsar encamped; but its name *Cissbury* plainly bespeaks it the work of king Cissa,[39] second Saxon king of these parts after his father Ella, when he landed with his

r. And those of viscount Cantalupe and earl Delaware 1761. which ended in the third earl John 1777.

Sussex, pp. 232–3. The ninth earl exchanged the manor of Halnaker for lands in Wherwell, Hants., in 1540. In the church there is the tomb of Sir Owen West (d. 1551), a member of the family. *B. of E. Hants.*, p. 650. The Cantelupe Chantry in Lincoln Cathedral was founded in 1355 for the tomb of Lord Cantelupe whose damaged effigy survives. *B. of E. Lincs.*, p. 113. It is surprising that Camden missed both Boxgrove and Halnaker: the modern itinerant should not.

38 The hill-fort of Cissbury was preceded by an undefended Iron Age dwelling-site of perhaps about 300 B.C. It was first fortified in about 250 B.C. with a massive rampart revetted with timber, surrounded by a ditch. Later in the Iron Age and during the Roman occupation of Britain, it was under the plough; and towards the end of the Roman period there was a relatively slight strengthening of the decayed ramparts, perhaps to make of them a refuge from barbarian raiders coming from the Germanic Continent. See *Arch. Sussex*, p. 230f., figs. 34, 76, pl. xxiii.

39 *Cissa* and his father *Ælle* (Camden's *Ella*) are mentioned in the entries of the *Anglo-Saxon Chronicle* which record the Saxon conquest of Sussex. They are: 477 (see p. 32, n. 36). 485: 'In this year *Ælle* fought with the Welsh near the bank of *Mearc rædes* stream.' This place has not been identified. 491: 'In this year *Ælle* and *Cissa* besieged *Andredes cester* [the Roman fortress at Pevensey] and slew all those who dwelt therein [and consequently] there was not even one Briton surviving there.' See also p. 53, n. 17.

brother Cimen,[40] and a considerable body of Saxons[41] at *Cimenshore*, so called from Cimen; which has now lost its name,[42] but appears by king Cedwalla's grant[43] of it to the church of Selsey, to have been near *Wittering*.[44] Another fortification called *Chenkbury*[45] is to be seen two miles from Cissbury.

Near the sea stands *Broadwater*,[46] the barony of the lords *Camoys*,[47] who have flourished from the time of Edward I. to the last age but one, when the estate came by James to the *Lewknors*[48] and *Radmilds*.[49] Of this family was John de Camois[50] son of lord Ralph de Camois, who, by an example as new in those times as in the present, "of his own free will gave and (to speak in the words of the parliament rolls)[51] demised his wife Margaret, daughter and heiress of John de Gaidesden,[52] to sir William Painel,[s][54] knight, and gave, granted, released, and quitted to him all the goods and chattels that he had, or might hereafter have, and also whatever was his of the same Margaret's goods and chattels with their appurtenances, so as that neither he nor any other in his name should or might make any demand or claim on the said Margaret for the goods and

s. With whom she had cohabited. Dugd. I. 767.[53]

40 *Cymenes ora* (Camden's 'Cimenshore') was apparently named after a man called *Cymen* (see p. 32, n. 36). *Wlencing*'s name occurs in a related form in the place-name Linchmere, Sussex; and the name *Cissa* is the first syllable of a few other place-names besides Chichester (e.g. Chessington, Surrey, and Chisbury, Wilts.). See *P.N. Sussex*, pp. xiiif., 10–11; and p. 32, n. 34 above. *Cissa*'s connection with Cissbury dates only from about Camden's day; it was earlier known as 'the old earthwork'. *P.N. Sussex*, pp. 197–8.

41 Camden's 'considerable body of Saxons' is not in the *Chronicle*, though it makes good sense, for the 'three ships' of the annal for 477 can have carried only a small force of invaders. In all probability the conquest of Sussex was effected by many ship-loads of land-hungry Saxons.

42 Not quite. See p. 32, n. 36, and *P.N. Sussex*, p. 83. The existing name Owers could represent a direct development from Old English *ōra*, 'shore', with the addition of a plural 's' quite late in the process of development towards the modern form.

43 See p. 35, n. 67.

44 At Cakeham, within the ancient territory of the *Wihtheringas* ('the people of *Wihthere*'), taking in the modern parishes of East and West Wittering, is a palace of the bishops of Chichester. Its earliest surviving parts are of C13. *B. of E. Sussex*, pp. 377–8.

45 Chanctonbury was *Changebury* in 1351. The etymology of this place-name is uncertain. See *P.N. Sussex*, pp. 53, 242, but cp. *Elements* II, 118, under *sengel*; and *Dic.*, p. 90, under Chancton(-bury). This hill-fort is of the Iron Age; see *Prehistoric Sussex*, pp. 69–70.

46 Broadwater is now engulfed by Worthing.

47 There are family monuments at Trotton, including one to Lady Margaret Camoys (d. 1310), 'the oldest existing female brass', which is figured in *Sussex Arch. Coll.* LXXX, 122, with a description on pp. 121 and 123. There, doubt is expressed as to which Margaret is intended. There is also a brass to Thomas Lord Camoys (d. 1419) and his wife, the widow of Hotspur, figured in *B. of E. Sussex*, p. 357.

48 The Lewknors had been at Brambletye and Bodiam (p. 66, n. 29). *Sussex Arch. Coll.* LXXII, 2–3. There is a damaged monument to Sir William Lewknor (d. 1616) at West Dean and others of late medieval date at Kingston Buci and Trotton. *B. of E. Sussex*, pp. 369, 252, 356.

49 This family was relatively undistinguished. Leland (*L.T.S.* IV, 92) may be referring to them when he says: 'Ther [in the chyrche of Petworth] lyith one Syr William Redmille a knight that dwellid, as I hard, in a log [lodge] of the great parke there.'

50 Sir John Camoys died in 1298.

51 The rolls of Parliament (*Rotuli Parliamentorum*), from the reign of Edward I onwards, began as very brief summaries of the legal and other business transacted there. They were first printed in late C18. See e.g. *Oxf. Hist.* IV, 347.

52 John de Gatesden the younger died in 1259.

53 On Dugdale, see p. 37, n. 88.

54 This was a family of much consequence. Ralph Paganell was given lands in Devon, Somerset, Yorks. and Lincs. soon after the Norman Conquest. *Oxf. Hist.* II, 620. Members of the same family held Newport Pagnell, Bucks., and Littleton Pannell, Wilts. The family name survives also in Boothby Pagnell, Lincs. Gervaise Painel (fl. 1189) was lord of Dudley Castle.

55 Rolls of Parliament for the 30th year of the reign of Edward I, i.e. 1301/1302. On the *Rotuli Parliamentorum* see *Oxf. Hist.* IV, 726, and see also p. 347 n.

56 This may be loosely translated: 'that he should have all her (possessions) with her'.

57 'the' is a misprint in Gough for 'she'. The sense seems to be that she was seeking possession of part of her first husband's goods which the law normally allows to a widow for life. Cp. the sense of 'dower house'.

58 This place eludes me. Torpel in Ufford, Northants., is unlikely as there are no recorded forms in '-hull'. *P.N. Nth.*, 1933, p. 224.

59 Gregory VII (1073–85).

60 Lanfranc was archbishop from 1070 to 1089.

61 Shoreham was merely a hamlet clustered round the old church until the early 1930s. It is now a disgrace. New Shoreham was carved out of the parish of Old Shoreham at some time between 1096 and 1103 by Philip de Braose. See *New Towns*, pp. 496–7.

62 The form 'Scoreham' is not given (*P.N. Sussex*, p. 246) for the Sussex place, but it is an early spelling for Shoreham, Kent, a name of identical origin. In Old English *scora* probably meant 'shore' or 'steep slope' and is related to the word-root found in 'shear, share, shire, score, shard', all of them having the implication of 'cut (off), separated'. See *Etym. Dic.*, pp. 818, 822.

63 The movement of shingle from west to east along the coast, together with great storms such as that of 1287 (p. 61, n. 95), caused obstruction of river mouths, an eastward shift of the outlets and a slowing down of the river current so that silt was deposited in the

Old Shoreham in 1645, engraved by Wenceslaus Hollar

chattels of the said Margaret henceforth for ever."* This was, according to the antient phrase *ut omnia sua secum haberet*,[56] packing her off bag and baggage. In consequence of this grant the[57] claiming dower in the manor of *Torpull*,[58] which belonged to John de Camois her first husband, occasioned a remarkable suit, which she lost; it being determined that "she had no right to dower from thence." I confess myself ashamed to mention this; but I see Pope Gregory[59] was not mistaken when he wrote to Lanfranc archbishop of Canterbury,[60] that he had heard there were certain persons in Scotland, that not only forsook but sold their wives, whereas in England they gave and granted them away.

Lower on the Shore is *Shoreham*,[61] antiently 'Scoreham',[62] which has gradually dwindled into a poor village, and is now called *Old Shoreham*, having given rise to another town of the same name, the greatest part of which is now destroyed and swallowed up by the sea, and the harbour has lost all its convenience by the sands driven up to the mouth of the river,[63] whereas in former ages ships used to come up under sail to

*Rot. Parl. 30 Edward I.[55]

estuary instead of being discharged into the sea. *Coastline* pp. 306–7; *Hist. Geog. Eng.*, pp. 302–3. The relative importance of Shoreham as a port, at least at one point in time, A.D. 1204, may be gauged from the table in *Oxf. Hist.* III, 96. Only Winchelsea and Chichester then had a larger volume of trade. See also *Sussex Arch. Coll.* LXXII, 168f.

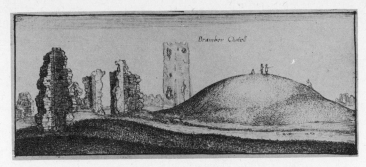
Bramber Castle, engraved by Wenceslaus Hollar

Brembre,[64] which is farther from the sea. This was formerly the castle of the *Breoses*,[65] being given by William I. to William de Breose, from whom are descended those Breoses who were lords of Gower and Brechin,[66] and from those in this county and Leicestershire spring the knightly family of the *Shirleys*.[67] Now the castle is nothing but a heap of ruins,[68] below which lies *Stening*,[69] called, if I mistake not, in Alfred's will, *Steningham*,[70] which has a good market on stated days.[71]

About three miles from the mouth, where when the Saxons first began to infest our coast, the *numerus exploratorum*[72] were stationed under the Roman emperors, but the masses of gravel that have rolled in have nearly choaked it up, seems to lie the old PORTUS ADURNI.[73] The name still almost intire, and the adjoining huts called *Portslade*, or *the way to the port*,[74] induce

64 Bramber is now a place to be hurried through – with the heavy traffic.

65 The Rape of Bramber is thought to have been created in about 1075, or if it already existed, it was handed over to William de Braose at about that time. *Arch. Journ.* CXVI, 229.

66 In John's reign a later William de Braose was 'far and away the strongest of the barons of the [Welsh] marches'. *Oxf. Hist.* III, 297. For long favoured by John, he fell unaccountably from favour in 1208 and fled. The king starved the wife and eldest son to death in prison. William died in 1211. See *King John*,

p. 204f. Besides his Sussex lordship of Bramber, he held Radnor, Brecon, Abergavenny, Barnstaple and Totnes, as well as Irish lands.

67 Sir John de Braose (d. 1426: brass in Wiston church) had no children surviving him 'and the estates passed to the Shirleys of Wiston, through Sir John's sister . . . , who had married Sir Hugh Shirley'. *Sussex Arch. Coll.* LXXX, 143–5; brass p. 144. According to Leland (*L.T.S.* IV, 93), this Shirley was 'Coferer of the Kinges House'. The effigy of a knight in the north wall of St John's, Southover, Lewes, is thought to be a monument of the Sir John who died in 1232. *B. of E.*

Sussex, p. 553. A late C13 tomb to Thomas Lord Braose is at Horsham. ibid., p. 243. Among their many manors in Sussex were Horsham, the Shorehams and Upper Beeding; and St Leonard's Forest was theirs.

68 A tall fragment of the tower-keep and fragments of the bailey wall are still visible. The castle was slighted in 1642 when the church also suffered. *B. of E. Sussex*, pp. 118, 119. For recent excavations see *Med. Arch.* XI, 285–6; XII, 178. The keep is perhaps of c. 1100. Sedgwick and Knepp were other de Braose strongholds in Sussex.

69 Steyning, for which see n. 71 below.

70 In the oldest surviving MS the text reads *æt Stæningum*. Camden presumably took this as a copyist's error for a place-name in *-ingahām*, of which there are so many in Sussex and the South-East generally. Its nominative was *Stæningas*, the meaning of which is doubtful (*P.N. Sussex*, pp. 234–6), but possibly 'people of the stony place (*stæne*)'. The form in the *Will* is in the Old English dative plural.

71 The Old Market House survives near the village centre. *B. of E. Sussex*, p. 340. Much of this place is very pleasing.

72 'A unit of scouts'. They were not stationed here, for there is no military site. However, a *Numerus Exploratum* at Walton is listed in the *Notitia Dignitatum*, an official list of the Roman forces in the Empire in C4.

73 See p. 36, n. 74.

74 Portslade meant '*Port*'s road (*ge-lād*)'. *P.N. Oxf.*, 1953, p. xlvi. *Port* occurs occasionally as a Saxon personal name (see my *Conquest of Wessex*, p. 145). On the clearly defined course of this road see *Prehistoric Sussex*, p. 116f.

75 Francis Wise (1695–1767), rector of Rotherfield Greys and librarian at Oxford, published several archaeological works. See the following note on the form of this place-name.

76 The text of Alfred's *Will* reads *æt Ēaderingtune* which is Arreton in Wight (*Dic.*, p. 12). Perhaps Camden had in mind Edburton, 3½ miles NNW of Portslade. This in C12 was *Eadburgetun*, 'Ēadburh's manor or farm', whereas Arreton was 'Ēadhere's manor'. If Camden had seen early MS forms for the Sussex place, he may well have been 'induced to place' (as he put it) the *Ēaderingtune* of the *Will* at Edburton. He tended to assume such identity between place-names even though they were only vaguely similar in spelling. See Introduction p. xxvii.

77 The widespread fear of French incursions c. 1538–43 led Henry VIII to embark on an elaborate system of coastal defence by means of artillery forts. There were over two dozen in all from Hull to Milford Haven, and many of them were built of material taken from the newly dissolved monasteries. Of these forts only Camber is in Sussex and Camden does not mention it; but he does refer to those in the Isle of Wight (Yarmouth, Cowes and Sandham, i.e. Sandown) and Hants. (Hurst and Calshot). Brighton was burned by the French in 1514. See 'The Coastal Defences of the South-East', by A. D. Saunders in *Arch. Journ.* CXXVI, 201–5, with map p. 202.

78 This is Brighton, of course. The middle element of the name began to fall out of use in C17. The form Brightemp*sted* does occur in early C17, but it is an error. The original spelling of the name would have been *Beorhthelmes tūn* meaning 'B's farm or manor'. Camden's older spelling with an 'a' is not included in the list of forms in *P.N. Sussex*, p. 291. The place-names Bright-

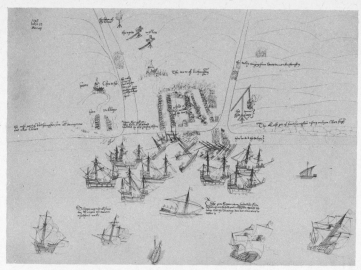

Brighton, the attack by the French in 1545

me to place it at the small village of *Ederington*,[t] [76] which Alfred gave to his younger son; not to mention how much the bold and open shore favours a descent here. For this reason our ancestors under Henry VIII. were here especially apprehensive of the French gallies, which hovering about our coast,[77] had burnt a cottage or two by surprize at *Brighthelmsted*,[78] antiently called 'Brighthealmes-tun', a neighbouring port.[79]

t. *Edingburne.* Wise.[75]

hampton, Oxon., and Brislington, Som., are identical with Brighton in meaning and etymology.

79 It was probably never a port, though erosion may have destroyed the anchorage. It was a fishing village until late C18, but Gough, in his *Additions* (p. 200) says that

It was once fortified with walls, of which traces remain. Queen Elizabeth is said to have built four gates, of which the eastern was taken down lately; and there was a flint wall to the sea three feet thick with port-holes, which, with the block-house built by Henry VIII. 1539, and a street of houses next the sea,

are all undermined by the sea, which has gained on the shore 50 yards within the memory of several middle-aged persons.

80 In its upper and middle reaches, at least, the river was known as *Midewinde* ('middle winding river'?) in records from C13, but it later received the name Ouse, probably from Old English *wāse*, 'mud, ooze'. *P.N. Sussex*, p. 6. This word occurs in the minor names of several shires (*Elements* II, 247), but the East Anglian and Yorks rivers Ouse probably have a different origin, possibly Celtic.

A few miles hence a nameless river[80] falls into the sea from the forest of St. Leonard near *Slaugham* the residence[81] of the *Coverts*[82] who were knights here t. Henry III.ᵘ

A little further hence from the sea stands *Lewes*, in a high situation, taking its name probably from the *meadows* called by the Saxons 'Leswa'.ˣ[85] For populousness and extent it may be ranked among the principal towns in the county.[86] "In the time of Edward the Confessor it paid six pounds four shillings gable[87] and toll.[88] The king had there 127 burghers. Their custom was if the king sent a fleet to sea without commanding it in person to levy on all to whomsoever the estate belonged twenty shillings for the use of those who did duty on board the ships. Whoever sold a horse in the town gave the governor[89] a piece of money, and the buyer another; a penny for an ox, and four pence for the buyer, wheresoever bought within the rape. Murder was amerced at seven shillings, adultery or rape at eight shillings and four pence the man, and the woman at as much; the king to have the adulterer, and the archbishop the woman.[90] [For retaking a man who run away eight shillings and four-pence]. On every new coinage each mint-master[91] pays twenty shillings. Of all these rates two thirds belonged to the king, and one to the earl."†ʸ[93] William de Warren earl of

u. Mr. Burrel has a curious MS. account of this family by St. Lo Kniveton.[83]

x. 'Læswe'.[84]

†Domesday book.

y. *Si rex ad mare custodiendum sine se mittere suos voluisset de omnibus hominibus cujuscunque terra fuisset colligebantur xx solidi & hos habebant qui in navibus arma custodiebant. Qui in burgo vendit equum præposito nummum, & qui emit, alium; de homine iiii denar. quocunque loco emat, &c.* Domesday, p. 26.[92]

---

81 Slaugham Place, an Elizabethan house, is in ruins. For a description of it, see *B. of E. Sussex*, p. 607.

82 This family was locally important in c16 and 17. There are brasses and monuments to their memory in the church. (Ibid.)

83 William Burrell (1732–96), lawyer, antiquary and M.P., became a baronet in 1789, too late for Gough to make a correction. Burrell collected material for a history of Sussex. There is a mural monument to him by Flaxman in West Grinstead church.

84 See n. 85 below on the form of this place-name.

85 Lewes takes its name from the hills near by. The name is to be derived from Old English *hlǣwas*. (*Elements* I, 249). Camden's 'Leswa' is not quoted among the early spellings (*P.N. Sussex*, p. 318) and the footnote *Læswe* presumably represents the dative singular of Old English *læs*, 'pasture, meadow-land'

(*Elements* II, 11), an entirely different word. In citing the form *Leswa* Camden seems to be justifying his preconception of what the place-name Lewes should mean.

86 It is still an important town and one in which to dawdle for many pleasing hours. However, the road-makers are threatening to cut it in pieces. There is a good plan in the Sussex *Little Guide*, p. 191; and see *B. of E. Sussex*, p. 549f.

87 A rent for land that may sometimes have been commuted for payment by service or in kind; but *gafol* could, in this context, be *haw-gafol*, levied on the *haga* or messuage, i.e. on the building as well as the land. See *Domesday Book and Beyond*, pp. 246–7; *Oxf. Hist.* II, 522f.

88 Market tolls on buying and selling.

89 Latin *praepositus* is the usual translation of English 'reeve', but here it is 'port (town)-reeve' (cp. sheriff, 'shire-reeve'), i.e. the chief officer who, later, with different responsibilities, was the mayor.

90 This means that the king is to receive the man's fine, the archbishop of Canterbury the woman's. *Domesday Book and Beyond*, p. 331. In n. 3 the author traces this division of the fine back to West Saxon law and forward to that of Henry II.

91 Æthelstan's laws issued at Grateley, Hants., between 924 and 939, par. 14.2, give the number of moneyers for each of 12 towns. For Lewes it was two. *E.H.D.* I, 384.

92 This is the original Latin beginning from '...if the king...' in the translation.

93 Elsewhere in Domesday Book this is called 'the earl's third penny'. *Oxf. Hist.* II, 527, and see n. 90 above. In later Saxon times the earls were appointed by the king, but the title tended to become hereditary. The earl usually received the third penny of the fines imposed by the shire-court. Ibid., pp. 539–40.

94 He became Earl of Surrey not long before his death 'in 1089. *Oxf. Hist.* II, 157, n. 5. He fought at Hastings and soon after built castles at Lewes, Reigate, Allington and Castle Acre, Norfolk. He also founded Cluniac priories at Castle Acre and Lewes and died in a siege of Pevensey Castle. He was buried in Lewes Priory and his leaden coffin and that of his wife were found in 1845 when a railway was being made across the site of the Priory. The coffins are now in St John the Baptist church, Southover, near by.

95 The castle was built c. 1100 with two shell keeps on mottes. Both mottes remain and one keep, as well as a gatehouse and some walling of the original structures. The surviving keep was strengthened in C13 with two turrets. The barbican is of C14. See *B. of E. Sussex*, pp. 554–5; plan in *Arch. Journ.* CXVI, 261.

96 The Priory was begun c. 1077 as the 'parent house of the Cluniac order in England' with a 'church nearly 450 feet long' based on the plans of that at Cluny. (Plan of Lewes Priory, *Arch. Journ.* CXVI, 259). The scraps of buildings remaining above ground are not very meaningful, but see *B. of E. Sussex*, pp. 550–51.

97 See *E.H.D.* II, no. 80, pp. 605–6 for a translation of this charter.

98 *Arch. Journ.* CXVI, 258:

At the Dissolution it was granted to Thomas Cromwell, and the method of his thorough destruction of the buildings is recorded in the report of John Potinari, the Italian engineer to whom he entrusted the work.

On the Sackvilles, Earls of Dorset, see pp. 66–7, nn. 38, 39. Cromwell was executed in 1540. Queen Elizabeth granted the site to Richard Baker and Richard Sackville (*Additions*, p. 201, citing Tanner).

Surrey[94] first built a castle here,[95] below which he dedicated a priory to St. Pancrace,[96] and filled it with Cluniac monks, "on account of the sanctity, devotion, and charity, which he found in the monastery of Clugni in Burgundy," as he expresses himself in his original charter of foundation,[97] while he lodged

Lewes Castle, with Lewes Priory in the foreground, in 1762, after Francis Grose

there with his wife in his pilgrimage. This has been since made the seat of the earl of Dorset.[98] Six churches[99] still remain in the town, amongst which, not far from the castle is a little ruined church[01] overgrown with briars, in whose walls on stones placed archwise are cut in antiquated characters these rude verses, implying that one *Magnus* of the blood royal of

99 Of these, three are within the line of the medieval walls of the town: (1) St John's sub Castro, rebuilt in 1839 a little to the south of the site described by Camden; (2) St Michael's, below the castle at its southern end, a medieval church with round tower, and later additions; and (3) All Saints, rebuilt in C19. Outside the town walls (*B. of E. Sussex*, p. 553) are (1) St Anne's, a good Norman building;

(2) St John the Baptist's, Southover, originally the Priory guest-house, with C18 tower and C19 additions, but especially worth visiting for the monuments to the founder of the Priory and his wife whose leaden coffins were found in 1845 (see n. 94); and (3) St Thomas Becket, Cliffe, medieval. *B. of E. Sussex*, pp. 551–4. St Mary's Lane took its name from another medieval church (*P.N. Sussex*, p. 319); and in

Denmark, who embraced a solitary life, was buried there. I have inserted them, imperfect as they are, and separated with the stones themselves.[02]

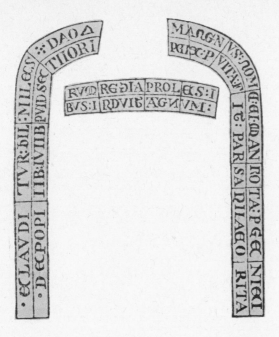

Which perhaps are to be read thus:

> Clauditur hic miles Danorum regia proles,
> Magnus nomen ei, magnæ nota progeniei.
> Deponens Magnum prudentior[z] induit agnum;
> Præpete pro vita fit parvulus anachorita.

>> Here lies a soldier good
>> Of Danish royal blood.
>> *Magnus* was once his name,
>> And like it *great* his fame.
>> His greatness laid aside,
>> An humbler life he tried,
>> Exchang'd for ruffian's prize
>> An hermit's simple guise.

In the Saxon times Athelstan having made a law that no money should be coined out of cities, appointed two mint-masters here.[03] In the Norman times it was distinguished by the fatal battle between Henry III. and his barons,[a] the success in the

z. It is now *Se moribus.*   a. M. Paris, p. 1350.[04]

the western part of the town there were, besides the surviving St Anne's, another St Mary's and a St Peter's (ibid., p. 320).

01 This church is of interest not only for the Magnus inscription (next note) but for its having been built within a Saxon fort, hence its name, St John's sub Castro (*Prehistoric Sussex*, p. 73). Other forts of the Burghal Hidage (*Med. Arch.* VIII, 74f.) in Sussex are possibly Hastings, East Hill (p. 58, n. 60 below) and Burpham, besides Chichester, whose Roman walls provided a ready-made fortress. For a sketch-plan of the Burpham fort, a 'fine promontory fort . . . built . . . by the Saxons as a fortress to guard the valley of the Arun, and so . . . in a sense the precursor of Arundel Castle', see *Earthwork of England*, fig. 212, p. 642. For another Sussex *burh*, no longer traceable, see *Med. Arch.* VIII, 81–5. On the town's later defences see *Med. Arch.* XII, 161–2.

02 The restored inscription, in Lombardic script, is on the south side of the church and is reproduced by Gough in his *Additions,* facing p. 193.

03 See p. 49, n. 91.

04 Matthew Paris (d. 1259), a chronicler at the monastery of St Alban's, revised and continued the *Chronica Majora* of his predecessor there, Roger of Wendover. Matthew is considered to have surpassed 'all the chroniclers of the twelfth century'. The position of St Alban's on a medieval main route, the Watling Street, kept him in touch with the court of Henry III and with the trends of political affairs including those of Europe. See *Camb. Hist. Eng. Lit.* I, 178–80. The *Chronica Majora* was readily available to Camden in the edition produced by Archbishop Parker in 1571.

05 For a modern brief account of the battle of Lewes (1264), see *Oxf. Hist.* IV, 189–90. The site of the battle is NG c. 397113.

06 Now called 'Decoy Pond'.

07 West Firle. The house, Firle Place, retains much of C16 as well as of mid-C18. *B. of E. Sussex*, pp. 624–5.

08 The Gages continued as loyal Catholics until early C18. Sir John Gage, in the time of Edward IV, married a St C ere, who held the manor of Heighton St Clere, the site of whose hall is in Firle Park. Firle has remained in the Gage family to the present day. See *Arch. Journ.* CXVI, 238–9; *B. of E. Sussex*, p. 624. There are brasses and tombs of the Gages in the church (ibid., p. 623) as well as at Framfield (ibid., p. 506).

09 'The manor was held by John de Sancto Claro in 1347, whence the place was alternatively known as St Cleres Manor.' *P.N. Sussex*, p. 361, and see previous note.

10 The Cuckmere seems not to have had a port. The name Cuckmere *Haven*, in use at least from mid-C14, probably misled Camden into thinking that there had been a harbour here; but a harbour (*hæfen*) capable of sheltering Anglo-Saxon ships, with their very shallow draft, was not necessarily capable of taking well-laden ships of post-Conquest times.

11 Spellings such as *Beuchef* (1274) or *Beaucheif* (1317) make it clear that Beachy (Head) is a name of French origin (*P.N. Sussex*, p. 427) and that it has nothing to do with the common noun 'beach', of which the etymology is uncertain (*Elements* I, 15; *Etym. Dic.*, p. 82). The 'Head' of Beachy Head is tautological, repeating the 'chef' of the name in its original French form.

12 *Peofensea*, with an 'o', is an abnormal spelling; the place-name

beginning of which proved the ruin of the king's party. For while his son Edward, having broke through some of the barons' troops, pursued them too far with the eagerness of a certain victory, the barons rallied again, and renewing the attack, gave the king's forces such a defeat that they obliged the king to offer hard terms of peace, and put his son Edward with other hostages into their hands.[05]

Thence by the side of the large lake[06] well stocked with fish near *Furle*[07] the seat of the *Gages*,[08] who derive great honour from marriage with a coheiress of the family of *St. Clare*,[09] we

Pevensey Castle, engraved by Wenceslaus Hollar

come to *Cuckmer*,[10] a very considerable harbour. Crossing over the promontory called *Beach* from its gravelly beach,[11] we come to *Pevensey*, antiently 'Peofensea',[12] by the Norm-

is composed of the Old English personal name *Pefen* and *ēg*, 'island or marsh' as the second element. *P.N. Sussex*, pp. 443–4. *Pevensel* is the Anglo-Norman form of the name, its ending comparable with that of e.g. Winchelsea (*Winchensel*, 1130 etc.). On this spelling see *E.P.N.S.* I, pt I, 94. The Roman fort was called *Andredesceaster* by the Saxons, and this they probably understood as '(Roman) fort of the Weald', for *Andred*, *Andredesleag*, and *Andredesweald* (*P.N. Sussex*, p. 1) were names they used for the great forest on the edge of which the fort stood. They took over the name

Andred from the Britons, though the Romano-British form of the name had been *Anderita* (*Lang. & Hist.*, p. 257, n.), and it appears as *Anderitos* (op. cit., p. 36) in the *Notitia Dignitatum* (on which see p. 47, n. 72). A tile found within the fort, stamped HON AUG ANDRIA, almost certainly refers to the Emperor (AUGustus) HONorius (395–423) in the first two abbreviations and to *Anderita* in the last. *Sussex Arch. Coll.* XXI, 112. The meaning of *Anderita* was probably 'the great fords'. See *Journ. Roman Studies* XXXVIII, 54, and *E.P.N.S. Journal* I, 50, s.n. *rid*.

ans[b] *Pevensel*, commonly called *Pemsey*,[16] formerly the castle[17] of Robert earl of Moreton[18] maternal brother to William the Conqueror,* afterwards of William[21] son of king Stephen, who resigned it to Henry II. from whom he received it with all the lands that had belonged to Richer de *Aquila*,[22] whence it

b. Pictav. 198.[13] Gemit. 286.[14] Ord. Vit. 500.[15]
*Flor. Worc. p. 452.[19] Robert de Monte, 1158.[20]

13 William of Poitiers, *Gesta Guillelmi ducis Normannorum et regis Anglorum* (Deeds of William Duke of the Normans and King of the English). See *Oxf. Hist.* II, 686–7. Poitiers was a member of the Conqueror's household.

14 William of Jumièges (fl. 1060) produced 'a sober and interesting chronicle' at the Norman monastery of that name. This work, entitled *Gesta Normannorum Ducum* (the exploits of the Norman Dukes), was published by La Société de l'histoire de Normandie. See *E.H.D.* II, 215–16, for a translation of the passage describing the invasion of England in 1066.

15 Ordericus Vitalis (1075–1143?), born in England of Norman parents, spent most of his life as a monk of St Evroult in Normandy. His *Historia Ecclesiastica* (Church History), which goes down to 1141, is valuable for its account of events after 1066, as seen from the cloister. See *Camb. Hist. Eng. Lit.* I, 163–4. *E.H.D.* II, 281f., gives his account, in translation, of the life and death of William the Conqueror.

16 It is so called in Speed's *Atlas* of 1627 and in documents of C16 and C17. This pronunciation (pemzi) was still current in 1930. *P.N. Sussex*, p. 443.

17 The castle's outer walls, enclosing nearly 10 acres, are Roman, probably of mid-C4, with south-west and east main gates and a postern on the north side. Ten solid bastions survive on which

great catapults could be mounted; but all of the south wall and a length of the north has collapsed. The fort (NG 645048) was on a peninsula, with a land approach only from the south-west; the east gate gave on to the harbour, which continued to be accessible until c. 1700, for the sea then came right up to the south and east walls; and there was marsh to the north. See *Coastline*, pp. 314–15. Excavations within them have shown that there were wooden buildings and at some time these were occupied by a *Numerus Albucorum* (a unit of Albuci) of whom we have no other information. After its capture in 491 (see p. 44, n. 39) and the massacre of the occupants, there was some ill-defined occupation by the Saxons. See the official guide *Pevensey Castle*, with photographs and a large-scale plan; also *B. of E. Sussex*, pp. 580–81. For excavations in the castle see *Med. Arch.* VI–VII, 323–4, and for excavations on the edge of the medieval port, ibid. XI, 209f. In the south-east corner of the Roman fort is a keep of c. 1100 and curtain walls with three towers and a gatehouse of c. 1250. 'The Roman walls withstood a siege by Stephen in 1147... [and] the castle was a refuge for the king's party after the battle of Lewes', in 1264. *Arch. Journ.* CXVI, 236. There were sieges also in 1088 and 1399. In C15 its strategic importance declined and it became eventually so ruinous that the intention of 1587 to put it into a state of defence against the Spanish Armada was abandoned;

but a small earthwork for a gun emplacement was dug midway along, but inside, the collapsed Roman south wall and its faint depression is still visible. The Napoleonic threat of invasion in the first decade of C19 was prepared for by the erection of Martello towers on the seaward side of the castle (*Arch. Journ.* CXVI, 236); and to meet the German threat of 1940, defences were concealed in the castle's ruins. Nowhere in Britain is there a spot which more fully draws past and present together.

18 Robert (d. 1091?) was given the county of Mortain by William in 1049. It was he who resisted Rufus at Pevensey in 1088 (see previous n.), where he built the castle c. 1100. Odo (d. 1097), Bishop of Bayeux in Normandy and earl of Kent, was his brother: the Conqueror, to whom he was second in power, his half-brother. He was disloyal to both the Conqueror and to Rufus. Odo was a patron of both learning and religion.

19 On Florence of Worcester, see p. 22, n. 58.

20 Alias Robert of Torigni, a Norman chronicler, who covered events from A.D. 1 to 1186. *Camb. Hist. Eng. Lit.* I, 172.

21 He was Stephen's second son who married the heiress of the Earl of Warenne (d. 1148) and gained thereby the Earl's great estates besides succeeding to those of his father, 'the honours of Lancaster, Eye and Boulogne and the county of Mortain'. In addition he held large estates in Sussex. He died in 1159. *Oxf. Hist.* III, 164–5.

22 The family of de Laigle held Pevensey with breaks for several generations, but the descent of the honour is nevertheless complicated. See the Official Guide to the Castle, p. 4. Engenulf de Laigle was slain at Hastings; Richer, his son, was killed in 1084. In 1229 Gilbert de Aquila founded Michelham Priory, of which the C15 gatehouse and some other parts survive (*B. of E. Sussex*, pp. 568–9). Camden omits it as he did Bayham Abbey, Wilmington Priory and about a dozen other religious houses, as well as Scotney and Camber castles.

23 The English word Eagle, the Latin Aquila and the French Laigle are equivalent in meaning. There is a Laigle on the river Risle, Département d'Orne, in Normandy, from which the family may have taken its name.

24 The Earl of Richmond mentioned here by Camden was Peter of Savoy 'who became Lord of Pevensey in 1246' and was probably the builder of the curtain walls and towers of the inner bailey of Pevensey Castle. See Official Guide, p. 11. He held lands in Bugei (now part of Ain) which was the north-western extremity of the County of Savoy from C10 to C13, and part of the Holy Roman Empire. He became Count of Savoy in 1263 and died in 1268. He was the uncle of Eleanor of Provence, queen of Henry III, and was for long an influential friend of that king. His predecessor in the Honour of Richmond was Peter de Dreux (Mauclerc), Count of Brittany (*Oxf. Hist.* IV, 92–4, 96–7), who played traitor to Henry III and lost his Honour of Richmond to Peter of Savoy. But Mauclerc seems to have had no connection with Pevensey in spite of Camden's reference to 'Breton earls of Richmond'.

25 This happened on a number of occasions between 1101 and mid C13. Thereafter 'It became the custom to grant the honour of Pevensey to the Queens of England...(who) became responsible for appointing

Herstmonceux Castle, engraved by J. Greig after H. Gastineau, published in 1815

had the name of the *Honor of the Eagle*.23 It was long the property of the crown, till Henry III. granted it to the Breton earls of Richmond,24 from whom it reverted to the crown.25 At present only the walls of the castle remain. Henry IV afterwards gave part of the honour of the Eagle to the *Pelham*26 family for their loyalty and bravery. Near it is *Herst*,27 among woods, whence it takes its name: the antient Saxons calling a wood 'Hyrst'.28 This soon after the Norman invasion was the seat of a noble family sometime called from it de *Herst*, till William son of Walleran de Herst, probably, according to the custom of that age from the place of his birth, assumed the

Constables of the castle.' Official Guide, p. 4.

26 Until Henry IV's accession, Sir John Pelham was merely Constable of the castle. In 1400 he was granted the castle and the honour and was custodian of distinguished prisoners such as Edward, Duke of York, and James I of Scotland. Official Guide, pp. 4–5. He held several great offices of state under Henry IV, but was deprived of them by Henry V. The Pelhams, nevertheless, became

a powerful family of which the Earls of Chichester and the Dukes of Newcastle of C18 are among the most famous.

27 The nucleus of the old village of Herstmonceux is near the church and castle, on which see *B. of E. Sussex*, p. 533f.

28 The probable meaning here was 'wooded hill' (*Elements* I, 276–7), which well suits the topography of the place.

54

name of *Monceaux*,† which this place still retains, being called from its owner *Herst Monceaux*.[30] From his descendants it came by inheritance to the *Fiennes*, who are also called *Fenis* and *Fienles* and descended from Ingelram de *Fienes* [31] who married the heiress of Pharamuse of Bologne. Of these Richard Finis was by Henry VI. "allowed, declared, and accounted" baron Dacre.‡ The same title Edward IV, honorary umpire between him and Humphry *Dacre*, "confirmed to the said Richard Fenis, and his heirs lawfully begotten," upon his marriage with Joan cousin and next heir to Thomas baron Dacre. From this time his posterity have enjoyed the title of barons Dacre, till the death[e] of the late George *Fenis* lord *Dacre* without issue, whose only sister and heiress Margaret was married to Sampson *Lennard*,[33] esq; a gentleman of singular virtue and politeness.

To return to Pevensey; William the Norman, (as I can here only repeat in brief what I before related more at large)[34] first put in here with his whole fleet,[d] and having landed his troops,

† Reg. mon. de Roberts bridge.[29]

‡ Pat. 37. H. VI.[32]

c. 1549.

d. Sept. 28. 1066. 3000 sail. Gemitic.[35] p. 286. Wace, p. 290.[36] The Chronicle of Normandy [37] says 907 great ships without reckoning small craft. See Lancelot Mem. de l'Acad. des Inscr. xii. 430. 12mo.[38]

---

29 Register of the Monastery of Robertsbridge. See p. 66, n. 28.

30 'The Munceus family are first associated with the place about the end of the 12th century.' *P.N. Sussex*, p. 480 and reference there. There is a place called Monceaux in Calvados, Normandy, from which the family may have taken its name.

31 Enguerrand de Fiennes (Ingram de Fenes) of the time of Henry III had ancestral ties with the Boulonnais. His descendant Sir Roger, who was at Agincourt (1415), built the Castle in mid C15. *Oxf. Hist.* IV, 545 n.; and see VI, 332–3, on the rising fortunes of the family in C15. In the church is a brass to Sir William Fiennes (d. 1402), the father of Sir Roger; and a canopied tomb of Thomas, 8th Lord Dacre (d. 1533) and his son,

Sir Thomas Fienes. *B. of E. Sussex*, p. 534. *Lamb.*, pp. 114, 138, records most improbably that a John Fynes was made Warden of the Cinque Ports and Constable of Dover Castle by William I. He records also that six of the Fienes family held those offices in later centuries. Ibid., pp. 114, 116. Leland (*L.T.S.* II, 14):

The Lord Dacres of the south is caullid Fines by propre name; and so is caullid the Lord Clinton. There was also in Henry the v. and the vi. tyme one of the Lord Sayes caullid Fynez. The last of the Lorde Sayes being in renowme [famous] was twise taken prisoner, wherby he was much punishid by the purse [through payments of ransom money]. Wherapon he was fain to lay most part of his land to morgage and solde clerely [outright] part of it. So that sins [that time] the name of the barony of Say is extinctid, but the heire males of the Lord Say in descent yet remainith caullid by the name of Fines.

32 An open (letter) of the 37th year of the reign of Henry VI, i.e. 1458/9.

33 Lennard was a genealogist and translator and, as a pursuivant of the College of Arms, well known to Camden. He died in 1615 and his tomb, besides those of other Lennards, is to be seen in Chevening church. *B. of E., W. Kent*, p. 202.

34 This was 'related more at large' in Camden's chapter headed 'Normans' (Gough's ed. of *Britannia*, pp. cxxi–cxxvii). Much of this had been written earlier and Camden observes (p. cxxii):

With the reader's leave I shall here subjoin an account of it [the Norman Conquest] which I drew up rather inaccurately and inattentively... when in the inexperience of youth... I formed a design of writing a history of England in Latin.

35 (William of) Jumièges. See n. 14 above and *The Normans*, p. 150.

36 Wace of Jersey (d. after 1171) was engaged by Henry II 'to compose an epic of the Dukes of Normandy which was completed in the "Roman de Rou" (Rollo) down to the battle of Tinchebrai' (1106). *Oxf. Hist.* III, 250; *Camb. Hist. Eng. Lit.* I, 264. His *Roman de Brut*, completed in 1155, is a poem based on the *History of the Kings of Britain*, by Geoffrey of Monmouth (1100?–1154). One of the main sources of this work was his own teeming imagination. He was the originator of many of the fictions concerning King Arthur. His work enjoyed great popularity in the Middle Ages and later and over 180 MSS of the work survive. A very readable translation is in the Penguin Classics.

37 Whichever of the chronicles may be intended here, it is not a significant source. For those that are significant for 1066 see *Oxf. Hist.* II, 686–7 and *The Normans*, pp. 265–7.

38 Lancelot, *Mémoires de l'Académie des Inscriptions et Belles-Lettres*, vol. xii, p. 430. This French Academy was founded in 1663.

39 Within the ramparts of the Roman fort. *Oxf. Hist.* II, 583.

40 This was hardly possible, for 'After a few days William transferred his fleet and army to Hastings' (ibid.). The *Chronicle of Battle Abbey* is the first to mention this burning of ships.

41 'Plain' is inappropriate as a description of this region of broken country (NG 745152 etc.), but the chroniclers had *planis* which, in medieval Latin, meant 'unwooded country'. See e.g. D. C. Douglas in *Norman Conquest*, p. 99, with sketch plan showing the relief of the battlefield, p. 96. For contemporary (c. 1070) Norman accounts of the invasion, by William of Jumièges and William of Poitiers, see *E.H.D.* II, 215–16, 224f.; and for an English account see MS 'D' of *A.S. Chron.*, p. 195f.

42 This was the battle of Stamfordbridge, Yorks., on which see *Oxf. Hist.* II, 580f. It took place on 25 September; the battle of Hastings on 14 October.

43 The *Chronicle*, MS 'D', says that Harold stationed his army 'at the grey apple-tree'. Moreover, 'Mr Camden mistakes *Epiton* for *Epitumium*, a word peculiar to Ordericus Vitalis, who uses it twice for a *field*, and makes the Conqueror on his death bed say that he had conferred the duchy of Normandy on his son Robert "*antequam in epitimio Senlac contra Heraldum certassem*", and Ordericus expressly calls the field of battle where William erected a church to the Trinity *Senlac*.' *Additions*, p. 203.

44 Eustace, Count of Boulogne, assisted in calming the panic of the retreating Normans at Senlac. He was the Conqueror's brother-in-law, but they quarrelled and Eustace rebelled with some support from the men of Kent. *Oxf. Hist.* II, 591.

45 The *Chronicle of Battle Abbey*, edited by Dugdale in *Monasticon*

and thrown up a strong rampart before his camp,[39] set fire to his ships,[40] that his whole dependence might be on his valor and all hope of safety on success: and immediately advanced to the plain [41] near Hastings, where the fate of England was determined, and the Anglo-Saxon empire brought to an end. For there our king Harold, though his army had suffered greatly in his late victory over the Danes,[42] and his soldiers were fatigued with their long march, on the 14th of October A.D. 1066 met the invader in a place called *Epiton*.[43] The Norman having sounded the charge, the battle continued some time with arrows; but afterwards when they came to close quarters it lasted much longer, till the English, who had stood the shock with great bravery, were briskly attacked by the Norman horse, who not being able to break their ranks, made a concerted but orderly retreat.[e] The English, thinking they were put to flight,[46] immediately quitted their ranks, and pursued them in disorder. The enemy facing about on a sudden renewed the attack with fresh vigour, and surrounding them on all sides repulsed them with great slaughter. The English retreating to higher ground, made a long resistance, till Harold himself was killed by an arrow: upon which they immediately gave way and fled.[47]

The Norman prince elated with his success founded in memory of this happy conclusion of the war, as a lasting trophy of the victory gained by the Normans, a monastery dedicated to St. Martin,[f] and called *De Bello*, or *Battel*,[49] on the

e. By the advice of Eustace earl of Bologne.[44] Chron. of Battel Ab. Mon. Ang. I. 311.[45]

f. *The Trinity*. Ord. Vit. 505.[48]

Anglicanum, vol. I, p. 311 (on which see p. 37, n. 88). The *Chronicon Monasterii de Bello* (ed. Brewer, 1846) must be distinguished from the Battle Abbey Roll which is no longer extant.

46 'Would it not be more correct to say that a "feigned retreat" was the recognized method by which chroniclers concealed the fact that the troops on their own side had run away?' *Norman Conquest*, p. 109; *Oxf. Hist.* II, 587; *The Normans*, pp. 51, 171–2 and notes.

47 There was, in fact, a final rally after this. *Oxf. Hist.* II, 587.

48 St Martin in fact. The reference is to Ordericus Vitalis (p. 53, n. 15).

49 The Abbey was called *De Bello* up to 1316, but also *La Batailge* almost from the beginning. *P.N. Sussex*, p. 495. It was consecrated in the presence of Rufus in 1095. Of the medieval structures there remain the gatehouse (c. 1340, *B. of E. Sussex*, pl. 30), the porter's lodge (Norman), the undercroft of the church (C14), the dormitory (C13, ibid., pl. 24) and fragments of walling and foundations. Much was absorbed by Sir Anthony Browne's house (n. 55), which incorporates the abbot's

56

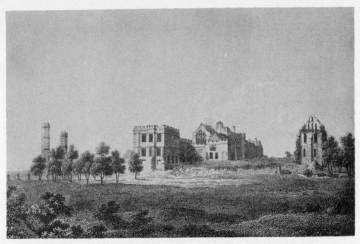

Battle Abbey, engraved by F. Hay after Francis Grose,
published in 1811

very spot where Harold covered with wounds breathed his last
among the thickest of his enemies. A town soon after sprung
up of the same name with the abbey, or to borrow the words
of the history of that house, "as the monastery increased, 115
houses were built round about it, which formed the town of
Battel."[50] In this town is a place called by a French name from
the blood shed there *Sangue Lac*,[51] which from the nature of
the soil looks red after a shower, whence William of Newburgh,[g] without any authority, writes, "The place where was
the greatest slaughter of the English fighting for their country
after a little shower sweats as it were fresh blood, as if to testify
openly and by demonstration of fact that the voice of so much
Christian blood yet cries out of the earth to the Lord."
William gave this monastery many and great privileges.
Among others, to quote the words of his charter, "If any
robber, or murderer, or other criminal, takes refuge in this
church, he shall not be molested, but suffered to escape. The
abbot of the church shall have power wherever he happens to
come to save a thief or robber from execution if he passes by at
the time."[53] Henry I. as his charter sets forth, "ordained here

g. I.1.[52]

lodge and some of the domestic
buildings of the Abbey, as well as
by the additions of 1857. See *B. of E.
Sussex*, pp. 404–7.

50 The development of a town at
the gates of an abbey is exemplified
at Abingdon, St Albans, Bury St
Edmunds and elsewhere. The

Conqueror endowed Battle Abbey
with a circular estate 3 miles in
diameter. The monks established
the town by laying out a market-
place at the Abbey gate, with
burgage plots surrounding it. See
New Towns, pp. 90–91, 130.

51 The name is most probably to
be derived from Old English *sand*
and *lacu* 'a stream'. 'Sanglake is
found in 1724 on a map of the
manor of Battle. As a matter of fact
the little stream here is of chalybeate
origin (i.e. impregnated with red
iron-salts) and does run red after
heavy rain.' *P.N. Sussex*, p. 499.

52 Book 1, section 1 of the *Historia
Rerum Anglicarum*. William of
Newburgh (1136–98?) was
educated at the Priory of Newburgh,
York. His *History of English Affairs*
covers the period from the Norman
Conquest until his own death and
is highly regarded as an historical
source. See *Camb. Hist. Eng. Lit.*1,
171–2.

53 The same King [William] graunted
to his Monkes of Battel, wrecke of the
Sea, falling upon Dengemarishe, a
portion of Wye, and willed further by
his Charter of donation, that if any fish
(called a Craspeis, that is, Crasse pisse, a
great roiall fishe, as whales or suche
other, which by the Lawe of Prerogative
perteined to the King himselfe) shoulde
happen to be taken there, that then the
Monkes shoulde have it wholly: And if
it fortuned to arrive in any other mans
land (lying betweene Horsmede, and
Withburne) that yet the Monkes should
enioy the whole tongue, and two third
partes of the rest of the body. (*Lamb.*,
p. 257.)

But the privilege probably most
valued by the Abbey was freedom
from episcopal jurisdiction. This
was enjoyed by only six or so of the
greater English foundations. See
Monastic Order in England, pp. 582,
589, 591. For the extent of the
burden imposed by the bishop's
visits see *The English Abbey*,
pp. 74–3.

54 This was granted in 1106.

55 He was the eldest son of Sir Anthony Browne (d. 1548) who received Battle Abbey and large grants of other monastic land in 1538. This included estates of Easebourne Priory, near Cowdray (p. 42, n. 19), Bayham Abbey on the border of Kent and Waverley in Surrey (p. 4, n. 25). The first Viscount Montague remained a Catholic and, in spite of his loyalty to Edward VI (and later to Elizabeth), he was imprisoned for recusancy in 1551. He later held high office in the state, having been made a viscount in 1554. Cowdray came to the Brownes in 1542 on the death of Sir Anthony's half-brother, the Earl of Southampton (a Fitzwilliam, not a Wriothesley). Montague's tomb, with effigies, is at Easebourne church, but disarranged in the move from Midhurst (*B. of E. Sussex*, p. 212). His father's monument, with effigies, is in Battle parish church (ibid., p. 408).

56 It was his father who built it.

57 On sanctuary and the successive measures to repress it see *English Wayfaring Life*, p. 77f.

58 Ashburnham was *Esburneham* etc., with an initial 'E' from C12 to early C14, but *Ashburnhame* from 1320 onwards, with occasional initial 'E' forms. The meaning was 'homestead or village by the stream overgrown with ash-trees'. *P.N. Sussex*, p. 477; *Elements* I, 226–7. The 'u' in Camden's spelling is an error. The village has gone, possibly destroyed when its site was emparked (cp. *Lost Villages*, p. 139f.); the house, built between 1813 and 1820, is largely gone as well, but there are Tudor lodges, that Camden may have seen, at Battle and Catsfield, where there are gates to the Park (*B. of E. Sussex*, pp. 409, 468). Ashburnham Forge and Furnace are reminders of the last of the Sussex ironworks, on which see p. 30, n. 15.

Hastings, engraved by Owen after F. W. L. Stockdale, published in 1814

a market on the Lord's day free of all toll."[54] But Anthony viscount *Montacute*,[55] who has lately built a very fine house here,[56] obtained an act of parliament to change the day. The rights of sanctuary in capital crimes have also been taken away from this and other places by parliament:[57] it being found that removing the fear of punishment served only to encourage crimes, and that the prospect of impunity was the greatest motive to guilt. Here is nothing else remarkable in this place or neighbourhood except *Esuburnham*,[58] which gives name to a family[59] the most antient of any in these parts.

Hastings before-mentioned, called in Saxon 'Hastingaceaster',[60] stands higher up on this coast. Some have ridiculously

59 This family was only locally famous until the Civil War of C17. Scotney Castle, Kent, started in 1377, was their main residence at that time (see *B. of E., W. Kent*, pp. 486–8). They acquired a barony in 1689 and an earldom in 1730. The title became extinct in 1924. There are family monuments in the church at Ashburnham. *B. of E. Sussex*, pp. 400–401.

60 *Hæstingaceaster*, with the digraph *æ*, occurs in MS 'D' of the *Chronicle* under the year 1050. It

meant 'fortification or town of the people of *Hǣsta*'. The modern name is from *Hsǣtingas* which, in various stages of development, is found from early times down to the present. It meant 'the people of *Hǣsta*' and was originally the name of an English tribe, later that of their territory. Cp. Sussex, Essex, Norfolk, etc. They were a people distinct from the South Saxons. *Oxf. Hist.* II, 18–19. In late C9 King Alfred built a fort here against the Danes (NG 833100?) (*Prehistoric Sussex*, p. 74); and the place was derived this name from our word *Haste*,[61] because Matthew Paris[62] tells us that "William the Conqueror run up a wooden fort at Hastings[63] in haste."[h] It seems rather to have taken its new name from Hasting[64] a Danish pirate,* who wherever he landed to ravage run up some castles,[66] as Asser Menevensis[i] relates of Beamflete[67] castle erected by him in Essex, and others at Apledor[68] and Middleton[69] in Kent. This place, in the time

h. His words (p. 3.) are *castellulum protinus construxit*, which Camden misquotes, *ligneum agiliter castrum statuit*. William staid here a fortnight, (Ib.) and here set up one of the wooden castles which he brought over with him. [See n. 63.]

*Hen. Hunt. VII. 211.[65]

i. Mr. Camden cites Asser by mistake for the Saxon Chronicle, p. 93. [See n. 67.]

important enough in C10 to have a mint (p. 60, n. 70). By the time of Domesday (1086), it had at least 24 burgesses and lesser men. In 1291 there were seven churches and it had become the chief of the Cinque Ports with six limbs (on which see p. 60, n. 74). For the varied history of Hastings see *New Towns*, p. 494. If *-cæster* had its usual Old English meaning, Hastings was preceded by a Roman town, perhaps a port for the shipment of iron from the seven or more Roman bloomeries in its immediate hinterland. Many small finds of Roman objects have been made in the neighbourhood of the present town. If there had indeed been a Roman port here, the erosion of the twin headlands sheltering the haven would have destroyed its vestiges. See O.S. *Map of Roman Britain*; *Coastline*, pp. 316–18. On the other hand, havens in the estuaries near Bodiam and Brede would have been more convenient and the Roman road from London to near Hastings, via Maidstone (*Roman Ways in the Weald*, p. 210f.), would also have reduced the need for a port at Hastings. The town still retains a few pleasing small neighbourhoods.

61 There is, in fact, an etymological link between 'haste' and the place-name Hastings. The common noun entered English via French, but was itself a French borrowing from German. Old English *hæst*, 'violence, fury', is from the same word-root as the German antecedent of 'haste' (*Etym. Dic.*, p. 430) and the place-name Hastings is probably formed from a personal name *Hæsta*, 'the violent one', a derivative of *hǣst* (*Dic.*, p. 213).

62 On Matthew Paris see p. 51, n. 04.

63 This fort is illustrated in *The Bayeux Tapestry*, pl. 52, 53. A motte and bailey castle is being built with what looks like a palisade of boards around the top of the motte. It lacks the wooden tower shown in the more permanent castles of Dinan (ibid., pl. 24), Dol (pl. 22) and Rennes (pl. 23). Traces of such a tower, in the form of large post-holes, were recovered in the excavation of the motte at Abinger, Surrey (*Arch. Journ.* CVII, 28f.). The motte of Hastings Castle is still a prominent feature of the site. Its excavation in 1968 yielded very little information. *Arch. Journ.* CXXV, 303–5. However, 'a sherd ... belonging to the conquest period' was found in the material used for the mound in its first phase.

64 The Dane 'Hasting' (*Hæsten* in Old English, *Hásteinn* in his own language, Old Norse) probably never came very near to Hastings, though in the campaigns beginning in 893 (correctly 892), as described in the *Chronicle*, the 'Great Army' of Danes, not *Hæsten*'s, probably harassed the Hastings hinterland. See *Parker Chronicle*, p. 41f.; *History of the Anglo-Saxons*, vol. II, pp. 655–64, with maps of the campaigns.

65 Henry of Huntingdon, *History of the English*, Bk VII. He 'was a facile writer, but a perfunctory historian'. See p. 22, n. 59.

66 In the *Chronicle* the forts are described as *geweorc*, 'encampments', which probably consisted of an area enclosed by a ditch, with an inner rampart surmounted by a palisade. Some vestiges of these earthworks may possibly survive near Milton (*Kent*, p. 33, n. 03); at Benfleet, Essex (NG c. 778860); and at Shoebury, Essex (NG c. 925845), where the War Department has done what it barbarously can to destroy the more considerable remains of the earthwork of 893. (Plan in *Earthwork of England*, p. 389, and see pp. 387–8.) An enclosure near Appledore, Kent, is an unlikely example, for which see p. 85, n. 11, *Kent*.

67 (*æt*) *Beamfleote* (Benfleet) is the form in MS 'A' of the *Chronicle* under the year 894 (in fact, 893). It is rendered 'tree-marked creek' in *P.N. Essex*, 1935, p. 142, but Ekwall's explanation of the meaning as 'stream with a beam, i.e. a foot-bridge' (*Dic.*, p. 35) is perhaps more likely.

68 Appledore meant, like its Devon counterpart, 'apple-tree'. See preceding n. 66.

69 This is Milton Regis, originally distinguished as the farm or settlement midway between Bobbing and Sittingbourne. See p. 33, nn. 99 ff., *Kent*.

70 See the Laws of King Æthelstan (924–39), grandson of Alfred, promulgated at Grateley, Hants., §14.2. *E.H.D.* I, 384.

71 For the beginnings of the Cinque Ports until early C13 see *Oxf. Hist.* III, 433f. and references there. Although it became the chief of the Ports in C12, it was the first to decline, for erosion of the cliff headlands that protected its harbour, and silting up of the small estuary, together deprived it of the shelter necessary for a medieval port. See *Hist. Geog. Eng.*, p. 302; *Coastline*, pp. 316–18 with map of Hastings in 1291.

72 The fleet required from all of the Cinque Ports was of 57 ships, as for example in 1294 (*Oxf. Hist.* IV, 655) and earlier (ibid., III, 433), but the full 57 was 'seldom forthcoming' in C14. (Ibid. V, 243, and see *E.H.D.* II, 968 for a charter of Henry II to Hastings.)

73 The twenty-first year of the reign of Edward I, i.e. 1292/3.

74 The members or limbs of Hastings were Grange (Kent), Pevensey, Seaford, and the lost places Northeye, near Pevensey, and Hydneye in the present marshes near Willingdon. See *Coastline*, pp. 314–316 for coastal changes here.

75 This was in return for much-valued privileges granted in the first place by Edward the Confessor. See *Oxf. Hist.* II, 426.

76 On the rape see p. 30, n. 18.

77 For 'honour' in this sense see p. 38, n. 96.

78 Robert, Count of Eu, was a cousin of the Conqueror and his trusted henchman. His Norman county was near the coast in the vicinity of Le Tréport.

79 Robert I was the Conqueror's father and sixth duke of Normandy. He ruled from 1027 until 1035 when he failed to return from a

of Athelstan, had its mint,[70] and is the "chief port" among the cinque ports,[71] which, with its members Winchelsey, Rhye, &c. is bound to furnish 21 ships [72] in time of war. If the reader is curious to see the form by which this and the other ports were obliged thus to serve the king in his wars at sea in return for the very considerable privileges granted them, take it in the very words in which it is recorded in the king's Exchequer.† "Hastings, with its members,[74] is to furnish at the king's summons 21 ships. In each ship are to be 21 stout experienced men well armed and equipped for the king's service; provided, however, the summons be issued on the king's part 40 days beforehand. And when the ships aforesaid with the men in them shall come to the place appointed, they shall abide there in the king's service 15 days at their own cost.[75] And if the king has need of their service after the 15 days aforesaid, or pleases to detain them there longer, the said ships, with their men, shall be waiting there in the king's service at the king's cost so long as the king pleases: the master to have six-pence *per* day, the constable six-pence *per* day, and each of the others three-pence *per* day."

The whole *rape*[76] and *honour*[77] of Hastings was held by the earls of *Augi*, commonly called *Ew* in Normandy,[78] descendants of a bastard son of Robert I. duke of Normandy[79] till Alicia, who, t. Henry III. was married to Ralph *d'Isson* in France,[80] and their issue lost their fine estate in England for *swearing allegiance*, as the Lawyer's phrase it, *to the king of France*.[81] But as in the early Norman times certain nobles in these parts were named *Hastings* and *de Hastings*, of whom Matthew de Hastings held the manor of *Grenocle*[82] on condition that "he found at this port an oar whenever the king passed over sea," ‡ so now the noble family of Hastings,[84] who are earls of Huntingdon, enjoy this title of Hastings; Edward IV.

† 21 *E . I.*[73]

‡ Inq. 5. *E. I.*[83]

pilgrimage to Jerusalem. The Conqueror was himself illegitimate.

80 Ralph d'Isson played no part in the history of England.

81 After the loss of Normandy by King John, those barons who had estates both there and in England were in a serious quandary as to their allegiance. See *Oxf. Hist.* III, 431–2.

82 This place has proved elusive.

83 An Inquisition post mortem of 1266/7. I.e. an inquiry 'into the land held by a tenant in chief at his death'. *Public Records*, p. 43.

84 The history of the Hastings family is complicated. By marriage they acquired the estates of the

having conferred it with certain royalties[85] as they are called on William Hasting[86] his chamberlain, who is commended by Comines[k] for refusing to give up a receipt for his yearly pension from Lewis XI.[88] the French king. "I will never suffer, said he, my receipt to appear among the accounts of the French treasury." But his unreserved favour with princes proved his ruin: for speaking too freely in the privy council to the tyrant Richard III. he was suddenly seized, and beheaded without trial.§ Nor must I omit that Henry VI. conferred on Thomas *Hoo*,[90] a worthy man whom he had made a knight of the garter, the title of baron *Hoo* and *Hastings*, whose daughters and heiresses were married to Geoffrey *Bollen*[91] (from whom queen Elizabeth was descended by the mother's side) Roger *Copley*,[92] J. *Carew*,[93] and John *Devenish*.[94]

The shore from hence retiring forms a bay, on which stands *Winchelsea*. The antient town of this name,[95] called by the

k. VI.2.[87]   § 26 H. VI.[89]

Botereaux, Molyns and Hungerford families. Mary, daughter of Sir Thomas Hungerford (beheaded 1469), a great heiress, married Edward Lord Hastings, who became the second Baron Hastings in 1483; and the third baron of this creation, George (d. 1545) was Baron Hastings of Hastings, Baron Hungerford, Botreaux and Molines. A favourite of Henry VIII, he was created Earl of Huntingdon in 1529. Camden's contemporary, the third Earl (1535–95) succeeded to the title in 1560. He had a claim on the throne through his mother. The remains of a fine brass to Sir Hugh Hastings (d. 1347) is to be seen in Elsing church, Norfolk (*Monumental Brasses*, pl. 4, 5). He was the elder son of the second Baron Hastings (of an earlier creation) who was also Baron Bergavenny and claimant to the Scottish throne (1262–1313). Leland (*L.T.S.* v, 4) has a very involved account of the marriage connections of the Hastings family. Monuments to them from C16 to C19 are in the parish church at Ashby-de-la-Zouch (*B. of E., Leics.*

and Rutland, p. 51) and their castle is near by. A chantry chapel, established 1503, commemorates the family at St George's, Windsor (*B. of E. Berks*, p. 276).

85 Manors or privileges.

86 William Hastings (1430?–83) was created a peer in 1461. For his death see *Oxf. Hist.* VI, 617–19.

87 Philippe de Commines (c. 1447–1511), whose *Mémoires* 'show him to be an historian of the first rank' (Larousse).

88 He ruled from 1461 to 1483.

89 The 26th year of the reign of Henry VI (i.e. 1447/8).

90 He died in 1485 and his tomb is in Horsham parish church. (*B. of E. Sussex*, pp. 243–4, but see p. 534.) Among his connections with Sussex were his acquisition of an interest in the manor of Pulborough and in lands near Chichester and Westbourne (*Sussex Arch. Coll.* LXXII, 262; LXXXIX, 139). He was made baron in 1447. His main residence was at Luton Hoo, Beds.

91 Sir Geoffrey Boleyn or Bullen, Lord Mayor of London, rebuilt Hever Castle, Kent, in 1453, retaining the late C14 core of the building. It was remodelled in about 1584 and restored, with alterations, in C20. (But see *B. of E., W. Kent*, p. 310f.) Camden does not mention this place. Sir Geoffrey was the great-grandfather of Queen Anne Boleyn (1507–36). He married Anne, daughter of Sir Thomas Hoo, in 1460. There is a brass to his son, Sir Thomas (d. 1539) at Hever, Kent (*Monumental Brasses*, pl. 11), and there are other family monuments at Blickling, Norfolk.

92 See p. 11, n. 62. This family also held the manor of Leigh, Surrey.

93 Camden, in speaking of Beddington, Surrey, mentions the fact that James Carew of that place 'married the daughter and co-heiress of the most noble baron Hoo'. See p. 19, n. 35.

94 As this is a rare name, it is possible that Richard Devenysshe, a lessee of land at Northolt, Middx, in 1534, was a descendant from this union. *Med. Arch.* v, 222.

95 It was situated on the left bank of the Rother (?NG c. 945185) where is a part of the parish of St Thomas the Apostle, Winchelsea. This was the dedication of a church in both the old and the new towns. During C13, war and more than usually rapid erosion by the sea, caused by a period of great storms, as well as 'the gradual rise in sea level which progressively weakened the site of the old town... made possible its final destruction in a single violent outburst' (in 1287). See *Coastline*, p. 325.

Leland gives interesting details (*L.T.S.* IV, 113–14):

The olde toune of Winchelsey of a vi. or 7. yeres together felle to a very soore and manifest ruine, be reason of olde [severe] rages of the se, and totally in the tyme of the aforesayde vi. or 7. yeres. In the space of these aforesayde yeres the people of Winchelsey made sute to kyng Edward the first for remedy and a new plot to set them a toun on. Whereapon the king sent thither John Kirkeby Bisshop of Ely and Treasorer of England, and vewid a plot to make the new toune of Winchelsey on, the wich was at that tyme a ground wher conies partely did resorte. Syr John Tregose a knight was the chief owner of it, and one Maurice and Bataille Abbey. The king compoundid with them: and so was there vii. score and tenne acres limited [allotted] to the new toune, whereof part is in the king mede withoute the toune, and part in hangging of the hille. Then in the tyme of the yere aforesayde the king set to his help in beginning and waulling New Winchelsey: and the inhabitantes of Olde Winchelsey tooke by a (litle and) a litle and buildid at the new towne. So that withyn the vi. or vii. yere afore expressid the new towne was metely [suitably] welle furnishid, and dayly after for a few yeres encreasid. But or xx. yeres were expired from the beginning of the building of New Winchelsey it was twise enterid by enemies, first by Frenchemen, that did much hurt in the toune, and secundarily by the Spaniards, that enterid by night at Fareley [Fairlight] aboute the midle way betwixt Winchelsey and Hastings. (Fareley wher the Hygh Steple is, 3. miles from Winchelsey). At this invasion the towne of Winchelsey was sore spoyled, and scant syns cam into pristine state of welth [and has hardly since that time regained its former prosperity]. For the commune voyce is that at that tyme wer xx. aldremen yn the toune marchauntes of good substaunce. In the toune as withyn the walles be 2. paroche chirches, and there were 2. colleges of freres. There is a litle withowt toune a paroche (chirch: but) that longith (to the liberte of Hastings). The name of the Finches hath beene of auncient tyme in estimation in Southsax about Winchelsey, and be al likelyhod rose by sum notable marchaunte of Winchelsey. For it is writen that Alarde and Finche Hereberte were capitaines in the Batel of Trade, and that Finche was sore woundid there. The Finches that be now say that theire propre name is Hereberte: and that with mariage of the Finche heyre they tooke Finches name and were

Winchelsea, the New Gate, engraved by T. Higham after F. W. L. Stockdale, published in 1817

Saxons 'Wincels-ea',[1] was swallowed up by the sea A.D. 1250.[97] at which time a great alteration was made in this coast[98] and the neighbouring coast of Kent; and the present town was built t. Edward I.[99] I shall present the reader with Thomas

l. q.d. *island* in a *corner*.[96]

caullid Finche Herebert, joining booth names. One Vincent Finch in Henry the 4. dayes recoverid of the king by a sute the manor of . . . by Winchelsey quarters. Alarde of Winchelsey was a man of estimation, and lyith buried yn Winchelsey. Oxenbridge of Southsax is heire by descent to this Alarde, and berith his armes.

96 The derivation of the place-name Winchelsea is probably from OE *wincel*, 'bend (in the coast)' and *ēg*, 'island, small peninsula, dry ground in a marsh'. *Elements* I, 147; II, 268. A derivation from a personal name *Wincel* and *ēa*, 'a stream', is less likely. The only other place-name for which this personal name has been postulated is Wigglesworth, Yorks., W. Riding, which in fact

stands beside bends in a stream. But cp. *Dic.*, p. 493; *Etym. Dic.*, s.n. wench, p. 999. Also *P.N. Glos.*, 1964, IV, 188, s.n. *wincel*; II, 29–30.

97 The storm of 1252 was only a contributory factor to the demise of the old town.

98 On the coastal changes in this region see *Coastline*, pp. 318–24, and maps, especially that on p. 326.

99 Planning of New Winchelsea began in 1281, but building-plots were not finally allocated until 1292. The pattern of planning within the walls was similar to that of the French new towns of the period (bastides), and the advice of an experienced man of Bordeaux was

Rye, the Ypres Tower, engraved by J. Greig after
F. W. L. Stockdale, published in 1817

Walsingham's[m] description of its situation. "It stands on a hill
very steep to the sea,[02] and overhanging the port; the road
leading from it to[03] which is not strait least[04] its great
declivity should make people tumble headlong as they walk
down, or oblige them to go up rather on all fours, but slopes
downwards, turning sometimes to one side and sometimes to
the other." It was first defended by earthworks,[05] afterwards
by stout walls,[06] and had scarce recovered itself when it was
plundered by the French and Spaniards,[n] and fell on a sudden to
decay by the retreat of the sea.[08] To the ruin of this place and the
favour of the sea the neighbouring town of *Rhie* owes it rise

m. [Left blank by Gough.][01]
n. 1377 and 1380. t. H.III. and R.II. The abbot of Battel and his monks
aiming to defend it were repulsed, and some of them slain. Walsingh. Hist.
Ang. 241. Ypod. 532.[07]

utilized in the layout. (See p. 22,
n. 02, *Kent.*) About 40 well-built
cellars of c. 1300 survive (*B. of E.
Sussex*, pl. 25b), intended probably
as places of storage for the produce
of Gascon vineyards. (On the
importance of this trade see *Hist.
Geog. Eng.*, p. 269f.) On the founding

of the town and its surviving
medieval remains see *Arch. Journ.*
CXVI, 255 and plan p. 256; *B. of E.
Sussex*, pp. 631–7 with plan p. 632;
Med. Arch. VIII, 268–9; and *New
Towns*, pp. 14–28. The Gascon
bastides are discussed in *Oxf. Hist.*
IV, 308–10 and *New Towns*, p. 348f.

A fine aerial photograph of the town
is to be found in *Med. Eng.*, fig. 95
and discussion pp. 221–5

To the modern visitor the place
hardly appears to be a decayed
medieval town; it is rather a village
where a pleasant hour or two may
be spent.

01 No note was in fact entered here
by Gough. On Walsingham see
n. 07 below.

02 This is apparent in pl. 75 of
Coastline.

03 The sense requires 'to' to be
omitted from the Gough
translation.

04 'least' is 'lest', i.e. 'for fear that .

05 Defensive earthworks are still
clearly visible at the southern end
of the town and along parts of its
western edge. About 300 yards
north-east of the medieval New
Gate are twin mounds astride an old
sunken road into the town.

06 A fragment survives in North
Street. Before that an earthen
rampart topped by a stockade had
sufficed until the French raids. See
notes 05 and 07. Three medieval
fortified gateways survive. *B. of E.
Sussex*, p. 635.

07 Winchelsea suffered from
French raids in 1337, 1359, 1380 and
1449. The effects of the burning of
the town are still visible in the
stonework of the church, which is
much reddened by fire in places.
The phrase 't. H.III' is an error for
'in the time of *Edward* III', who died
in 1377. The Abbot of Battle was
Hamo and the year 1331. The two
works by Walsingham are *Historia
Anglicana*, which covers the period
1272 to 1422, and *Ypodigma
Neustriae*, a summary of English
history from 911 to 1419. *Oxf. Hist.*
V, 544; VI, 699–700.

08 The retreat of the sea from New
Winchelsea was probably but one
aspect of the processes of erosion
and deposition that produced

Dungeness. See *Coastline*, p. 323f.
The position of Winchelsea 'at the
natural outlet of the Weald made it
the greatest exporter of timber and
fuel in England throughout the
Middle Ages' (*Hist. Geog. Eng.*,
p. 322). Yet 'by the mid-fourteenth
century holdings (in the town) had
become vacant' and the harbour had
silted up by Elizabeth's time. *B. of E.
Sussex*, pp. 622–3.

09 For coastal changes affecting the
port of Rye see *Coastline*, p. 318f.
and maps pp. 328, 329.

10 The word 'present' is a slip.
The castle of Rye was built in C13,
but its name commemorates
William of Ypres (d. 1165), who
was 'chief military commander' of
King Stephen and captain of that
king's Flemish mercenaries. *Oxf.
Hist.* III, 140, 321. He was grandson
of the Count of Flanders. For his
loyal service in England and
Normandy, Stephen rewarded him
with the revenues of royal manors
in Kent, but did not, as is sometimes
stated, create him Earl of Kent. The
earldom of Kent in Camden's day
was held by the family of Grey of
Ruthin.

11 On the origin of the Cinque
Ports see p. 60, n. 71. Rye and
Winchelsea were already associated
with the Ports by the end of C12;
for their trade in early C13 see *Oxf.
Hist.* III, 96. In 1449 Tenterden,
Kent, with its quay at Smallhythe,
became a 'limb' of Rye. These two
ports could communicate by water
round the Isle of Oxney. See maps
in *Coastline*, p. 328. On Rye's origin
see *New Towns*, pp. 495–6.

12 Fragments survive of the walls
and the Landgate of C14 is virtually
complete. *B. of E. Sussex*, pp. 596,
598.

13 Rye is still a very attractive small
town in spite of a somewhat self-
conscious 'quaintness' produced for
the edification of tourists. Nevertheless, it is one of the places in

or rather recovery,[09] for that it was antiently considerable and
fortified by William the present earl of Kent is evident from
the present tower[10] and the privileges it enjoys in common
with the cinque ports.[11] Its nearness to Winchelsea or the
retreat of the sea occasioned it to lie in former ages long
neglected: but on the decline of that place in the reign of
Edward III. who fortified this with walls,[12] it began to revive,
and in the last age the sea, to make ample amends for the
mischief it had done it, broke in so violently in a great storm
as to make the harbour very commodious, to which another
storm in my time has not a little contributed. From this time
it became tolerably well furnished with inhabitants and buildings,[13] and is considerable for its fishery and marine.[14] It is now
the most frequented passage[15] to Normandy. Whether it has
its name from *Rive* a Norman word for a *Bank* I cannot determine. But as it is often called in the records by the Latin name
Ripa, and the people who bring fish from hence are called
Ripiers, I rather incline to that opinion, which I should more
readily do were it certain the French used this word for the *sea
shore* as Pliny° does *Ripa*.[17]

o. IX. 15. Add also Florus IV. 28. Columella I. 5.[16]

south-east England that is worthy
of a lengthy sojourn.

14 'marine' here must mean
'shipping'.

15 'passage' means 'crossing' here.

16 Bk 9, §15 of Pliny's 'Natural
History'. Pliny the Elder (A.D. 23–
79), administrator, soldier and
admiral, died during the eruption
of Vesuvius when Pompeii and
Herculaneum were overwhelmed.
Of his writings only the encyclopedic
On Natural History has survived.
Pliny claimed that its 37 books
contained 20,000 noteworthy facts
drawn from over 470 authors.
Medieval writers relied on it
extensively and it would have been
known to Camden in one of the
several editions published on the
Continent from 1473 onwards.
Florus could be either the Roman
historian of A.D. 11, Lucius Annaeus
Florus, or his part-contemporary,

Annaeus Florus, the poet. Lucius
Junius Moderatus Columella wrote
a work (c. A.D. 65), *De Re Rustica*, on
agriculture and rural occupations.

17 The usual Latinized form of the
name is *Ria* or *Rya* (C12–C13).
Middle English forms are *Rie* or
Rye. In these instances 'i' and 'y'
are interchangeable. The meaning
was 'at the island', which, in Old
English, had been '*æt thǣre īege*'.
This became *atter īe*, then, as one
word, *atterīe*, in Middle English.
Lastly, when separated, the syllables
were wrongly divided, giving *atte
Rie*. Even now, with the sea
withdrawn over two miles, there is
water on three sides of what had
been a true island. It had been part
of the manor of *Hrammeslege* in the
late Saxon period. *P.N. Sussex*,
pp. vi–vii, 536. In modern French
'la rive' is restricted in meaning to
the 'banks of a river, pool or lake',

Into this harbour falls the river *Rother* or *Rither*,[18] which rising at *Ritheramfeld* (for so the Saxons called our present *Rotherfold*),[19] runs through *Burgwash*, antiently *Burghersh*,[20] which had lords of its own name, among whom was that Bartholomew Burgwash, an eminent man in his time, who, by his prudence in embassies and bravery in the wars of Aquitaine, rose to the rank of a baron of the realm, was one of the first founders of the order of the garter, constable of Dover castle, and warden of the cinque ports.[21] Nor did his son[22] of the same name degenerate from his character, but flourished in the highest splendor, and left an only daughter, who married into the family of *Le Despenser*, from whom descended a long series of noble persons.[23] *Echingham* in this neighbourhood had also its own baron William de Echingham,[24] t. Edward II. whose ancestors were Seneschals[25] of this *rape*; but the estate came at last by the heirs female to the barons *Windsor*[26] and

but 'le rivage' is applied also to the 'sea-shore'. Both words are from Latin *ripa*, which only rarely (as in Horace) was applied to the shores of the sea.

18 There are two rivers Rother flowing through Sussex, the western rising in Hants. and joining the Arun near Pulborough (p. 42, n. 18), and the eastern rising near Mayfield in Sussex, its estuary at Rye. Both of these names are back-formations (cp. Arun, p. 36, n. 78). The western is formed from the old hundred-name of Rotherbridge ('cattle-bridge') of which the moot-place was near Rotherbridge Farm; and the eastern from the village-name Rotherfield ('unwooded land for cattle'), which was also the meeting-place of a hundred. See *Eng. River N.*, p. 347; *P.N. Sussex*, pp. 7, 99, 123, 372, 376. The Old English word *hrīther/hrȳther*, 'oxen, cattle', occurs later as *rither*, *rother* or *ruther* according to dialect. *Elements* I, 265. There are Rotherfields in both Oxon. and Hants. of the same derivation.

19 Both of these forms are erroneous. The Old English one

seems to be a misreading of *Hrytheranfelda* in King Alfred's *Will*, which Camden frequently quotes; but that form, in any case, 'would (also) seem to be a bad one'. *P.N. Sussex*, p. 377. The substitution of '-fold' for '-feld' is by analogy with the numerous -fold names, of which most are in the north-west of the county and in the neighbouring areas of Surrey. Ibid., p. 550.

20 In Camden's day, and even now, Burwash is pronounced 'Burrish' or 'Berrish'. The first element is OE *burh*, 'fortress, stronghold', and the second *ersc*, 'a ploughed or stubble field', a word that went out of common use early. *Elements* I, 157–8; *P.N. Sussex*, p. 461.

21 The elder Bartholomew Burghersh, Baron Burghersh, died in 1355. In the 1330s he was 'one of the most important English officials on the Continent' and 'became one of (Edward III's) closest confidants'. *Oxf. Hist.* V, 117, 152.

22 He died in 1369 and it was probably his tomb that was recently discovered during the course of excavations at Walsingham Priory,

Norfolk. *Arch. Journ.* CXXV, 277f. and pl. XXVII, B. He is mentioned a number of times by Froissart in his *Chronicles*. See Brereton's translation, p. 484, for references, and especially p. 163: 'That fine soldier and great English baron....' He was a founder-member of the Order of the Garter, as Camden noted in his account of St George's Chapel, Windsor. There are Burghersh tombs of 1340 and 1355 in Lincoln Cathedral. *B. of E. Lincs.*, p. 113.

23 The elder Hugh le Despencer (1262–1326) became Earl of Winchester in 1322. Both he and his son, Hugh the younger, were executed in the same year. Thomas le Despencer, great-grandson of the younger Hugh, was created Earl of Gloucester in 1397, but was degraded from his earldom in 1399 and beheaded in 1400. Yet another Hugh le Despencer was 'governor' of the young Prince Hal (*Oxf. Hist.* VI, 44–5). But Camden is here probably thinking of Mary Fane or Vane, lineal heir of the 'Nevilles lords of Abergavenny and le Despenser...to whom and her heirs king James [I] in his first parliament ...gave...the...rank of baroness le Despenser.' So Camden, under Mereworth, Kent (see pp. 17–18, *Kent*).

24 There are several brasses to the Etchingham family in the parish church of which one, which is now headless, commemorates its founder who died in 1389. See *Sussex Arch. Coll.* LXXXVII, 201, 204; *B. of E. Sussex*, p. 497; *Brass Rubbings*, pl. 20b. The fortified gatehouse to their manor, of c. 1300, at Glottenham has recently been excavated. *Med. Arch.* X, 204; XII, 195–6; XIII, 194.

25 'Seneschals' here must mean governors of the rape.

26 Under Bradenham, Bucks., Camden remarks that that place was, in his day, the chief seat of the

Windsors. The most famous person of this name was Sir William of Windsor (d. 1384), who became viceroy of Ireland and was one of the chief suppressors of the Peasants' Revolt of 1381. However, his main claim to valour was his marriage with Alice Perrers. *Oxf. Hist.* v, 386–7.

27 The Tyrwhits remained a predominantly Lincolnshire family.

28 The Abbey was founded by *Robert* and not Alfred de St Martin in 1176, and it was Robert who gave his name to the bridge. *P.N. Sussex*, p. 459. The recognizable ruins of the Abbey consist of a crypt, the arches of a chapel, and some walling, mostly of c13. *B. of E. Sussex*, p. 589. On a recent excavation see *Med. Arch.* XI, 276. On the Dissolution of 1538, it was given to Sir William Sidney, grandfather of the poet Sir Philip.

29 Bodiam Castle 'is the ideal picture of the powerful, wholly planned castle'. *B. of E. Sussex*, p. 419; and for a description see the pages following. It was begun soon after 1386 and 'was the last great purely military castle to be reared in England'. W. Douglas Simpson, *Sussex Arch. Coll.* LXXII, 85. For the church and castle see ibid., p. 69f. and small plan, p. 70; *B. of E. Sussex*, pp. 419–21 and pl. 31b; on its planning, *Arch. Journ.* CXX, 231f., with plans. To the modern visitor the castle in its setting of water, trees, grass and hills, is surely one of the most lovely in Europe. Leland (*L.T.S.* IV, 68) says of it no more than 'therby ys an old castel cawled Bodiam'.

30 See p. 45, n. 48.

31 For the descent of the manor from the Bodehams to the Wardeux family, of whom the heiress Elizabeth married Sir Edward Dalyngrigge, builder of Bodiam Castle, see *Sussex Arch. Coll.* LXXII, 83. Sir Edward was a Sussex man, of Dalling Ridge,

Bodiam Castle, engraved by T. Bonnor after F. W. L. Stockdale, published in 1813

the *Tirwhits*.[27] Afterwards the Rother in three channels passes under *Roberts bridge*, where Alured de St. Martin. t. Henry II. built a monastery;[28] and passing by *Bodiam*,[29] a castle belonging to the antient and famous family of the *Lewknors*,[30] built by the *Dalegrigs*,[31] falls here into the sea.

Having thus surveyed the coast of Sussex, nothing remains to be mentioned in the inland parts but extensive woods and forests, the remains of the antient *Sylva Anderida*.[32] Among which, to begin from the west, the most considerable are the Forest of *Arundel*,[33] *St. Leonard's* forest,[34] *Word* forest,[35] *Ashdown* forest,[36] (below which last lies *Buckhurst*,[P][38] the seat of the

p. In Witham parish.[37]

Forest Row, and served in the French wars (ibid., p. 83) and became 'warden' of London. *Oxf. Hist.* v, 467. A brass to a Dallingridge of c14 is in Fletching church. *B. of E. Sussex*, p. 501, figured on p. 502.

32 The Wealden forest. See p. 29, n. 07 and p. 52, n. 12.

33 It is not to be found on modern maps nor apparently has such a forest been referred to by that name in recent centuries. The still heavily

wooded region to the north of Midhurst and Petworth is possibly what is meant.

34 The region round NG 230320.

35 This is Worth Forest around NG 310350.

36 Around NG 460300. For a summary history of the area see *Arch. Journ.* CXVI, 243.

37 Withyham. See n. 39 below.

38 The house of the Sackvilles is now mainly represented by its early

antient family of the Sacviles,[39] from which sprung Thomas Sacvile, a person equally eminent for prudence and nobility, created by queen Elizabeth in my time baron Buckhurst, made a privy counsellor, knight of the garter, and lord treasurer of England, and lately by king James, earl of Dorset,q) *Waterdown* forest,[41] and that of *Dallington*,[42] the least of all.

Sussex had five earls of the family of *Albiney*,[43] called also earls of Arundel. The first of these, *William* de Albiney, son of William cupbearer[44] to king Henry I. and lord of Buckenham[45] in Norfolk, bore G. a lion rampant Or,[46] and was sometimes styled earl of Arundel, sometimes earl of Chichester, from his chief residence being at those places.r He had by Adeliza[48] daughter of Godfrey the bearded, duke of Lorrain and Brabant, widow of king Henry I, *William*, second earl of Sussex and Arundel,s father of *William* the third earl, who, by Mabil sister and coheiress of Ranulph last earl of Chester,[50] had *William* the fourth earl,t and *Hugh* the 5th earl,u who both died

q. He was born 1536, and died suddenly at the council board 1608.[40]

r. He died 1176, and was buried at Wymondham, Norfolk. Dugd. I. 120.[47]

s. He died returning from the siege of Damieta, 1222, and was buried at Wymondham. Ib.[49]

t. He died 18 Henry III.[51]

u. He died 1243, and was buried at Wymondham. Ib.[52]

Tudor gatehouse. See *B. of E. Sussex*, p. 639.

Leland (*L.T.S.* IV, 82):

The auncientest house of the Sachvilles that now livith is at Bukhurste yn Southesax by the Forest of Waterdoun, a 2. or 3. miles from Rotherfield also in Southsax. This Sacheville is a man of a 300. li. land by the yere. Sacheville of Bedforde that was grome-porter cam out of this house. [A groom-porter was an officer of the royal household who regulated gaming.] And so did Sacheville of Blechingle in the quarters by Rigate, a man now of a 40. markes of landes by the yere.

39 Buckhurst is said to have come into the hands of the Sackvilles in the time of Henry II. The fact that even by 1074 a certain Herbrand de Saqueville was holding land in England suggests that he came over

with the Conqueror. Sir Richard (d. 1566), related to the Boleyns (p. 61, n. 91), was the first of them to acquire national fame. Thomas (1536–1608), the poet, also held high office and was made Earl of Dorset in 1604. Later titles held by the family include the earldom of Middlesex, the dukedom of Dorset and the viscounty of Sackville. Some of the family tombs are at Withyham, close to Buckhurst, for which see *Arch. Journ.* CXVI, 244, with plan; *B. of E. Sussex*, p. 638, pl. 44a. There is also a Sackville tomb at Westhampnett (ibid., p. 373). In 1601 the family acquired Brambletye Manor (*Sussex Arch. Coll.* LXXII, 3f.) and in 1603 Knole, which became their principal residence. See *Knole and the Sackvilles*.

40 See previous note.

41 'In Waterdown forest is Eridge' (i.e. around NG 560350), *Additions*, p. 205.

42 Around NG 645207 etc.

43 See p. 37, n. 89; p. 38, n. 93.

44 He was sometimes given the title *Pincerna*, in relation to his office.

45 He was building a castle at New Buckenham, Norfolk (NG 084904) from about 1145 to 1150. *B. of E., N.W. and S. Nfk.*, p. 268.

46 For his coat of arms he bore a golden (*or*) lion rampant (i.e. upright supported on one hind paw, the forepaws widely separated) on a field (background) of red (*gules*). These arms were perhaps borne by his descendants rather than him, for as 'cup-bearer to king Henry I' (1100–1135), he lived at a time when heraldry was only first beginning to appear. *Oxf. Hist.* III, 24.

47 In Wymondham Abbey, founded in 1107 by William d'Albini (presumably 'Pincerna', n. 44) as a Benedictine priory of which the church was for the use of the parish. No Albini monuments survive. The final reference in this note is to William Dugdale's *Baronage of England*, on which see p. 37, n. 88.

48 Adeliza (d. 1151), daughter of Godfrey of Louvain, was Henry I's second queen whom he married in 1121. See p. 37, n. 83.

49 The capture of Damietta in the Nile delta in 1219 was a main incident in the Fourth Crusade.

50 Ranulph de Blundevill in 1216 was 'the greatest baron of the realm' (*Oxf. Hist.* III, 2), and besides Chester, he held the earldom of Lincoln (ibid., p. 20, n. 1). On his death in 1232, the earldom of Chester went to the son of his eldest sister, the Earl of Huntingdon (ibid., p. 197, n. 1).

51 I.e. 1233/4.

52 See n. 47 above.

53 He was licensed to build Tattershall Castle in 1231. *B. of E. Lincs.*, p. 390.

54 See above p. 38, as well as Gough's note *n* to the same passage and p. 42, n. 13.

55 Someries Castle, near Luton, Beds., was a house of the de Someries.

56 This Norman family seems to have had little part in Sussex history or, indeed, in the history of England in the Middle Ages. The Scottish form of the name is Mowat.

57 See p. 38, and p. 42, n. 13.

58 Sir Robert Radcliffe (1483–1542) became Earl of Sussex in 1529. The fifth Earl (1569?–1629) succeeded to the title in 1593.

59 The FitzWalter family became prominent in about 1100; a Robert FitzWalter acquired the manor of Little Dunmow, Norfolk, in about 1105. A later Robert, Lord Fitz-Walter, leader of the barons' army against King John in 1215, was Lord of Dunmow and of Baynard's Castle in London, recently excavated, both of which lordships he succeeded to in 1198, according to Stow (*Survey of London*, p. 57), who sets out the Baron's rights in the City of London in detail (ibid., pp. 58–60). This Robert, too, was at the siege of Damietta (p. 67, n. 49). By 1394, and probably earlier, the family estates included manors throughout East Anglia (*Oxf. Hist.* VI, 7). The first Earl's father, John (1452?–96), became the first Baron FitzWalter in 1485. He was beheaded for his part in the Warbeck conspiracy (*Oxf. Hist.* VII, 122). At the Dissolution of the monasteries, the first Earl of Sussex (see preceding note) acquired Little Dunmow Priory (*English Monks and the Suppression of the Monasteries*, p. 58) in the church of which are to be seen fine effigies on the tombs of his ancestors. *B. of E. Essex*, p. 253, pl. 33a.

without issue, and four daughters married to Robert lord of *Tateshall*,[53] John *Fitz Alan*,[54] Roger *de Somery*,[55] and Robert *de Montalt*.[56] The title of Arundel was afterwards revived, as I before observed, in the *Fitz Alans*,[57] but that of Sussex lay in a manner lost till the present age, which has seen five *Radcliffes*[58] of the most noble family of Fitz Walter[59] (descended from the Clares)[60] ennobled by it, viz. *Robert*[x] created earl of Sussex by Henry VIII. who married [first] Elizabeth daughter of Henry Stafford duke of Buckingham,[62] and had by her *Henry* second earl,[y][64] who had by Elizabeth[z] daughter of Thomas Howard

x. He died 1542, and was buried in St. Laurence Pountney church, London. The monument with the figures of the three earls richly habited was brought to Boreham in Essex, and placed in the chapel there erected by earl Thomas; by the decay of which it was lately in imminent danger of being destroyed.[61]

y. He died 1583, and was buried at Boreham, Essex. Dugd. II. 286.[63]

z. She died 1589, and was buried in St. Paul's chapel, Westminster abbey. Ib.[65]

60 The founder of this great family in England was Richard Fitz-Gilbert (or Richard of Tonbridge), son of Count Gilbert of Brionne, a companion of the Conqueror at Senlac, who 'was lord of Clare in Suffolk and of a great fee in East Anglia and the eastern Midlands. Baldwin his brother was lord of Okehampton in Devon.' *Oxf. Hist.* II, 622, 624 and n. 2. He died c. 1090.

Gilbert and Roger of Clare were with Rufus when he was killed in 1100 and were probably in conspiracy with Henry I also present, to bring about Rufus's death (*Oxf. Hist.* III, 113–14). In C12 the family played a large part in the history of Wales (ibid., p. 290) and that of Ireland (ibid., p. 305f.). They acquired the earldoms of Clare, Hertford, Pembroke and Striguil, and Gloucester. Some time after the death of 'Strongbow', conqueror of Ireland, in 1176, his daughter and heiress was given by Richard I as wife to William Marshall, who with her acquired the earldom of Pembroke and Striguil. The death of Gilbert de Clare, Earl of Clare,

Gloucester and Hertford in 1314 at Bannockburn resulted in the final break-up of the Honour of Clare among his three sisters. *Oxf. Hist.* V, 40, 58–9. See also p. 14, n. 89; p. 25, n. 95.

61 At Boreham are the alabaster effigies of three of the earls on one tomb-chest. According to *B. of E. Essex*, p. 82, they died in 1542, 1567 and 1583; according to J. Charles Cox, a fine scholar (*Little Guide, Essex*, p. 66), they died in 1542, 1556 and 1583. Other sources give the second earl's death as in 1557. New Hall, in Boreham parish, a house built by Henry VIII, was given by Queen Elizabeth to the third Earl of Sussex.

62 Henry was the second Duke of Buckingham (1454?–83). He was beheaded by Richard III for open rebellion.

63 See n. 61. The reference is explained on p. 37, n. 88.

64 1506?–57. He was captain-general and a privy councillor under Mary Tudor.

65 See *B. of E. London* I, 375.

duke of Norfolk,[66] *Thomas,*[67] who was lord chamberlain to queen Elizabeth, and died without issue; a most illustrious hero, to whose united prudence in the cabinet[68] and valor in the field England and Ireland[69] can jointly bear witness. He was succeeded by his brother *Henry,*[a] and he by his only son *Robert,*[71] a most honourable youth, now living.

This county contains 312 parishes.

a. He died 1593, and was buried at Boreham. Ib.[70]

THE KINGDOM OF THE
SOUTH SAXONS

So much for Sussex; which was with Surrey the residence of the REGNI;[72] afterwards the kingdom of the SOUTH SAXONS, called in Saxon 'Suth seaxan-ric',[a] founded 32 years after the arrival of the Saxons[74] by Ælla, who, according to Bede, was first[75] among the kings of the Angles in all the southern provinces separated on this side the Humber and the boundaries contiguous thereto. Their first Christian king was Edilwalch, baptized in the presence of Wulpher king of Mercia,[76] who was his godfather, and in token of his adopting him gave him two provinces, the Isle of Wight and the country of the Meanvari.[77] Three hundred and six years after the foundation of this kingdom, Aldin the last king being slain by Ina,[78] it fell entirely under the dominion of the West Saxons.

a. 'Suth seaxna-ric'[73]

66 The second (1443–1524), third (1473–1554) and fourth (1536–72) dukes of Norfolk were named Thomas Howard.

67 Thomas (1526?–83), like his father the second Earl of Sussex, supported Queen Mary. He became lord-deputy of Ireland in 1556 and under Elizabeth was made Lord President of the North.

68 The council chamber in which the chief royal officers met.

69 As lord-deputy of Ireland he acquired a great reputation for statesmanship.

70 There seems to be no monument to him at Boreham.

71 1569?–1629. He gained some distinction in affairs and as a patron of writers.

72 On the *Regni* (*Regnenses*) see p. 1, n. 01.

73 More usual than this form cited by Gough is *Suth Seaxlond,* as given in the *Chronicle,* under the years 773, 897.

74 Tradition, as recorded in the *Anglo-Saxon Chronicle,* placed the first landing of the South Saxons in 477 (see p. 32, n. 36), but no event concerning Sussex is recorded until 32 years later.

75 Camden's 'first' is explained by Bede (*E.H.* II, 5), who speaks of the death of *Æthelberht* of Kent in 616 and says of him that he was the third to become over-king (*Bretwalda,* 'ruler of Britain', *Chronicle,* under the year 827) of all the provinces of the English south of the Humber. The first to hold this *imperium* was *Ælle,* king of the South Saxons. On the significance of this title see *Oxf. Hist.* II, 33f.

76 See p. 35, n. 63.

77 The *Meonware,* 'dwellers along the river Meon'.

78 The *Chronicle,* under the year 722, records that *Ealdbriht* (MS 'E'; *Ăldbryht,* MS 'A') the exile fled into Surrey and Sussex. Under 725 it is said that Ine fought against the South Saxons and there slew *Ealdberht* the prince whom he had banished. No king of the South Saxons called *Aldin* is known. On the Sussex dynasties see *Oxf. Hist.* II, 58, 207.

APPENDIX

THE ANGLO-SAXON CHRONICLE 'is the most fruitful source for the history of England between Bede and the Norman Conquest'. Seven manuscripts survive, but after the annal for 915 they show much independence of each other. The earlier annals are derived from Bede, from oral traditions, some of which had been preserved in verse, and from brief notices of events in Latin. The assembly of the material began in the late ninth century and the chronicles were continued year by year with the addition of the main events in national or regional history inscribed soon after they had occurred.

MS 'A' The Parker Chronicle, was kept at Winchester in C10 and was transferred to Canterbury in C11. It ends in 1070. It is now Corpus Christi College, Cambridge, MS 173, folios 1–32.

MS 'B' A copy of a lost MS which may have been at Abingdon. The copy was made c. A.D. 1000 and kept at Canterbury, but it was not continued after 977. It is now British Museum, Cotton MS Tiberius A vi, folios 1–34.

MS 'C' Another copy of the lost Abingdon Chronicle, made in mid C11 and continued to 1066. It is now British Museum, Cotton MS Tiberius B i, folios 115–64.

MS 'D' A copy made in mid C11 of a lost chronicle kept in northern England, which had been expanded by matter taken from Bede and other northern sources. The copy was sent to the diocese of Worcester and there continued to 1079. It is now British Museum, Cotton MS Tiberius B iv.

MS 'E' The Laud or Peterborough Chronicle has affinities with 'D'. It was sent to Canterbury and remained there until after 1066. A copy of it was made at Peterborough in about 1122. It was continued until 1154. It is now Bodleian MS Laud 636.

MS 'F' A twelfth-century epitome of 'E', in English and Latin, made at Canterbury after the Conquest. It ends in the middle of the annal for 1058; how much is lost is unknown. It is now British Museum, Cotton MS Domitian A viii.

See *Oxf. Hist.* II, 679–84; G. N. Garmonsway (trans.), *The Anglo-Saxon Chronicle*, 1953; *E.H.D.* I, 109f.; *E.H.D.* II, 107f.; and C. Plummer, *Two of the Saxon Chronicles Parallel*, 2 vols., 1892 and 1899.

THE VENERABLE BEDE (673–735) lived most of his life in the Northumbrian monastery of Jarrow. Among his numerous works, all in Latin, the *Historia Ecclesiastica Gentis Anglorum* (Ecclesiastical History of the English People), finished in 731, stands out as the work of a great scholar. Stenton has said that 'in regard to all the normal substance of history his work can be judged as strictly as any historical writing of any time'. His collection of evidence and critical use of it is essentially

71

modern. See e.g. *Oxf. Hist.* II, 185f.; the translation of 1955 by L. Sherley-Price; and the standard edition of all Bede's historical works: *Venerabilis Baedae Opera Historica*, ed. C. Plummer, 2 vols., 1896.

DOMESDAY BOOK is the record of an agrarian survey made in 1086, 'deliberately planned so as to reveal the territorial basis on which English feudalism rested'. 'As an ordered description of a national economy it is unique among the records of the medieval world.' See *Oxf. Hist.* II, 644f. and references there; and *E.H.D.* II, 198f.

EDMUND GIBSON (1669–1748) was librarian at Lambeth Palace, archdeacon of Surrey, bishop of Lincoln and then of London (1723–48). He declined the archbishopric of Canterbury a year before his death. Among his published works were editions of the *Saxon Chronicle* (1692), of Camden's *Britannia* (1695) and some of Spelman's writings. His *Britannia* appeared when he was only twenty-six years of age, the translation being undertaken by a team of scholars each of whom had local knowledge of the shire allotted to him. As editor he revised and collated their contributions. Their work has a directness and strength of idiom characteristic of the English language of the time, but, as Gough was to find, they were not always accurate in their renderings of Camden's Latin. The work has been republished in facsimile in 1971.

RICHARD GOUGH (1735–1809) made antiquarian excursions through the English shires over a period of twenty years. Most noteworthy among his publications is the translation of Camden's *Britannia* (1789) incorporating most of what was worthy of preservation from the editions of Holland and Gibson, and with lengthy additions of his own. It has been considered the best of the translations and, as a whole, is the truest rendering of Camden's original Latin text.

PHILEMON HOLLAND (1552–1637) qualified in medicine, but is remembered for his translations of Livy (1600), Pliny's *Natural History* (1601), Plutarch, Suetonius, Ammianus Marcellinus and other authors, as well as for his somewhat free rendering of Camden's *Britannia* of 1610. See D. Bush, *English Literature in the Earlier Seventeenth Century*, 1945, pp. 57 and 553.

JOHN LELAND (1506?–52) was the first of the modern English antiquaries. He journeyed round England from about 1535 to 1543, noting antiquities of all kinds with the intention of writing a great work on ancient Britain (*De Antiquitate Britannica*). He was fanatical in his patriotism and in his belief in the truth of Geoffrey of Monmouth's *History of the Kings of Britain*. In 1544 he made a savage attack in print on Polydore Vergil's *Anglica Historica* (1534), which had cast doubt on Geoffrey's accuracy. One of Camden's few acknowledgements to Leland cites the Latin poem *Cygnea Cantio* (1545), which opens with a description of the Thames between Oxford and Greenwich as seen from the river. The *Itinerary*, a record of his travels, survives in a fragmentary state, much of it consisting of hasty jottings in need of revision and some of them repetitive of earlier notes. Intermixed with them are extracts from medieval chronicles that would have provided sources for his history, as the topographical notes would have been the basis of his observations on antiquities. He became insane in 1550 before he could organize his vast mass of materials and write them up. Although he lacked aesthetic sense, he was well endowed with sharp powers of visual awareness and a directness of expression that make his *Itinerary* fascinating to read. Camden used this work very considerably in the *Britannia*, but without acknowledgement. The *Itinerary* was first published in 1710 and again in 1906–7 by L. Toulmin Smith. This edition was reproduced in 1964 and in cheaper format in 1971. For Leland's life and a discussion of his work see the foreword by T. D. Kendrick. His *Collec-*

tanea, which consists of extracts from histories, annals, chronicles, and of genealogical notes and catalogues of manuscripts, was published in 1715. The MS had been available to Camden.

JOHN STOW (1525–1605), a London tailor, was the acquaintance or friend of most of his contemporary antiquaries and his valuable library, like Sir Robert Cotton's, was open to them. Unworldly and industrious in his researches, he experienced great poverty late in life, yet persevered in his main task, *The Survey of London*, published first in 1598 and enlarged in 1603. His earlier publications were of medieval chronicles, including that of the so-called Matthew of Westminster in 1567; the *Chronica Majora* of Matthew Paris in 1571; and the *Historia Anglicana* of Thomas of Walsingham in 1574. The *Survey* was edited in 1908 by C. L. Kingsford with full critical apparatus, and in 1912 by H. B. Wheatley in a cheap edition.

GENERAL BIBLIOGRAPHY

JOURNALS

Antiquity
> I, 1927, 'Ancient Writers on Britain', C.E. Stevens, 189f.
> XII, 1938, 'Nennius and the Twenty-Eight Cities of Britain', K. Jackson, 44f.
> XXXII, 1959

Archaeologia
> XCIII, 1949, 'The British Section of the Ravenna Cosmography', I. A. Richmond and O. G. S. Crawford

Archaeological Journal
> XCII, 1935, 'Norman Domestic Architecture', M. Wood, 167f.
> XCVII, 1940, 'The British Sections of the Notitia Dignitatum', C.E. Stevens, 125f.
> CV, 1950, Supplement, 'Thirteenth Century Domestic Architecture in England', M. Wood
> CXII, 1955, 'The Reorganisation of the Defences of Romano-British Towns in the Fourth Century', P. Corder, 20f.
> CXIX, 1962, 'A Survey of Romano-British Town Defences of the Early and Middle Second Century', J. Wacher, 103f.
> CXXIII, 1966, 'Medieval Undercrofts and Town Houses', P. A. Faulkner, 120f.
> CXXIV, 1967, 'The Origins of the Castle in England', B. K. Davison, 202f.
> CXXVI, 1969, 'The Coastal Defences of the South-East', A. D. Saunders, 201f.
> CXXVI, 1969, 'An Historian's Approach to the Origins of the Castle in England', R. A. Brown, 131f.

Archaeological News Letter, 1948–65

Essays and Studies of the English Association
> XIX, 1934, 'English Names and Old English Heathenism', B. Dickins, 148f.

Journal of Roman Studies
> XXXVIII, 1948, 'On some Romano-British Place-Names', K. Jackson, 54f.

Medieval Archaeology
> II, 1958, 'Medieval Inquisitions and the Archaeologist', M. Beresford, 171f.
> V, 1961, 'Soldiers and Settlers in Britain, fourth to fifth century . . .', S. C. Hawkes and G. C. Dunning, 1f.
> VI–VII, 1962–3, 'Medieval English town-house plans', W. Pantin, 202f.
> VIII, 1964, 'The Unidentified Forts of the Burghal Hidage', N. Brooks, 74f.
> XIII, 1969, 'The Burghal Hidage: The Establishment of a Text', D. Hill, 84f.
> XIV, 1970, 'The Later Pre-Conquest Boroughs and their Defences', G. A. Ralegh Radford, 83f.

Proceedings of the British Academy
> 1935, 'Laurence Nowell and the Discovery of England in Tudor Times', R. Flower, 47f.
> 1951, 'William Camden and the *Britannia*', S. Piggott, 199f.

BOOKS AND MAPS

Abbeys: An Introduction to the Religious Houses of England and Wales, R. Gilyard-Beer, 1959
Ancient Burial-Mounds of England, The, L. V. Grinsell, 2nd edn, 1953
Anglo-Saxon Charters, P. H. Sawyer, 1968
Anglo-Saxon Chronicle, The, G. N. Garmonsway (trans.), 1953
Archaeology and Place-Names and History, F. T. Wainwright, 1962
Archaeology in the Field, O. G. S. Crawford, 1952
Archaeology of Roman Britain, The, R. G. Collingwood and I. A. Richmond, 2nd edn, 1969
Archaeology of South-East England, An, G. J. Copley, 1958
Archaeology of Wessex, The, L. V. Grinsell, 1958
Architecture in Britain, 1530–1830, J. Summerson, revised edn, 1955
Asser's Life of King Alfred, W. H. Stevenson (ed.), 1904

Atlas of Tudor England and Wales, An (from John Speed's Pocket Atlas of 1627), E. G. R. Taylor, 1951

Bayeux Tapestry, The, E. Maclagan, 1943

Bede, His Life and Writings, A. Hamilton Thompson (ed.), 1935: 'Bede as Historian', W. Levison

Beginnings of English Society, The, D. Whitelock, 1952

Black Death, The, P. Ziegler, 1969

Brass Rubbings (Victoria and Albert Museum), M. Clayton, 1968

Britannia, a History of Roman Britain, S. Frere, 1967

British Antiquity, T. D. Kendrick, 1950

British Islands and their Vegetation, The, A. G. Tansley, 2 vols., revised edn, 1949

British Plants and their Uses, H. L. Edlin, 1951

Buildings of England, The, N. Pevsner (ed.), 1951–74. Complete in forty-six volumes. Page references are to first editions.

Cambridge History of English Literature, Vol. I: 'From the Beginnings to the Cycles of Romance', A. W. Ward and A. R. Waller (eds.), 1949

Castles: An Introduction to the Castles of England and Wales, B. H. St J. O'Neil, 1953

Catalogue of Manuscripts containing Anglo-Saxon, N. R. Ker, 1957

Chronica Majora, Matthew Paris (H. R. Luard ed.), 7 vols., 1872–84

Chronicles, J. Froissart (G. Brereton sel., ed., trans.), 1968

Chronicles and Annals, R. L. Poole, 1926

Chronicon ex Chronicis, Florence of Worcester (B. Thorpe ed.), 2 vols., 1848–9

Chronicon Monasterii de Abingdon, J. Stevenson (ed.), 2 vols., 1858

Coastline of England and Wales, The, J. A. Steers, 1946

Complete Atlas of the British Isles (Reader's Digest), n.d.

Concise Oxford Dictionary of English Place-Names, The, E. Ekwall, 2nd edn, 1940

Conquest of Gaul, The, Caesar (S. A. Handford trans.), 1951

Conquest of Wessex in the Sixth Century, The, G. J. Copley, 1954

Crawford Collection of Early Charters and Documents, W. H. Stevenson and A. S. Napier (eds.), 1895

Dark Age Britain, D. B. Harden (ed.), 1956: 'The Jutes of Kent', C. F. C. Hawkes; 'Romano-Saxon Pottery', J. N. L. Myres; 'Coinage in Britain in the Fifth and Sixth Centuries', C. H. V. Sutherland

Description of England, The, W. Harrison (G. Edelen ed.), 1969

Development of the Castle in England and Wales, The, F. M. Stenton, 1933

Dictionary of National Biography: The Beginnings to 1900, 22 vols., 1885–1900

Domesday Book and Beyond, F. Maitland, 1897

Domesday Geography of South-East England, The, H. C. Darby and E. M. J. Campbell (eds.), 1962

Earthwork of England, A. H. Allcroft, 1908

Ecclesiastical History of the English People, The, Bede (C. Plummer ed.), 2 vols., 1896

England in the Late Middle Ages, A. R. Myers, 1952

England of Elizabeth, The, A. L. Rowse, 1950

English Abbey, The, H. Crossley, 2nd edn, 1939

English Church Monuments (1510–1840), K. A. Esdaile, 1946

English Coins, G. C. Brooke, 3rd edn, 1950

English Field Systems, H. L. Gray, 1915

English Historical Documents, Vol. I: c. A.D. 500–1042, D. Whitelock (ed.), 1955: 'The Anglo-Saxon Laws', 327f.; 'Charters', 337f. – Vol. II: 1042–1189, D. C. Douglas and G. W. Greenaway (eds.), 1953 – Vol. III: 1189–1327, H. Rothwell (ed.), 1975

English Hundred-Names, The, O. S. Anderson, 1934

English Hundred-Names, The: The South-Eastern Counties, O. S. Anderson, 1939

English Literature in the Earlier Seventeenth Century, D. Bush, 1945

English Monks and the Suppression of the Monasteries, G. Baskerville, 1937

English Place-Name Elements, A. H. Smith, 2 vols., 1956

English Place-Name Society

Vol. I, pt I: *Introduction to the Survey of English Place-Names*, A. Mawer and F. M. Stenton (eds.), 1933: 'The Celtic Element', E. Ekwall, 15f.; 'The English Element', F. M. Stenton, 36f.; 'The Feudal Element', J. Tait, 115f.; 'The French Element', R. E. Zachrisson, 93f.; 'Personal Names in Place-Names', F. M. Stenton, 165f.; 'Place-Names and Archaeology', O. G. S. Crawford, 143f.

Vol. I, pt II: *The Chief Elements in English Place-Names* superseded by *English Place-Name Elements*, q.v.

Journal 1, 1968–9, to v, 1973.

English Place-Names, K. Cameron, 1961

English Place-Names and Their Origins, G. J. Copley, revised edn, 1971

English Pronouncing Dictionary, D. Jones, 11th ed., 1958

English River-Names, E. Ekwall, 1928

English Scholars, D. C. Douglas, 2nd edn, 1951

English Society in the Early Middle Ages, D. Stenton, 1951

English Wayfaring Life in the Middle Ages, J. J. Jusserand, 4th edn, 1950

Flores Historiarum, Roger of Wendover {H. O. Coxe ed.), 5 vols., 1841–4

Gesta Guillelmi ducis Normannorum et regis Anglorum, William of Poitiers (R. Foreville ed.), 1952

Gesta Normannorum Ducum, William of Jumièges (J. Marx ed.), 1914

Gesta Pontificum Anglorum, William of Malmesbury (N. Hamilton ed.), 1870

Gesta Regum Anglorum and *Historia Novella*, William of Malmesbury (W. Stubbs ed.), 1887–9

Handbook of British Chronology, M. Powicke and E. B. Fryde, 2nd edn, 1961

Handbook of Greek and Latin Palaeography, E. M. Thompson, 1906

Heraldry in England, A. Wagner, 1946

Historia Anglicana, Thomas of Walsingham (H. T. Riley ed.), 2 vols., 1863

Historia Anglorum, Henry of Huntingdon (T. Arnold ed.), 1879

Historia Ecclesiastica, Ordericus Vitalis (A. le Prevost ed.), 1838–55

Historia Minor (Historia Anglorum), Matthew Paris (F. H. Madden ed.), 3 vols., 1866–9

Historia Novorum in Anglia, Eadmer (M. Rule ed.), 1884

Historic Towns and Cities in the British Isles . . . from earliest times to 1800, Vol. I, M. D. Lobel (ed.), 1969

Historical Geography of England before A.D. 1800, An, H. C. Darby (ed.), 1951: 'Camden's England', E. G. R. Taylor; 'Leland's England', E. G. R. Taylor; 'Medieval Trade: Eastern Ports', R. A. Pelham

History of the Anglo-Saxons, A, R. H. Hodgkin, 2 vols., 2nd edn, 1939

History of the English Church and People, Bede (L. Sherley-Price trans.), 1955

History of the Kings of Britain, The, Geoffrey of Monmouth (L. Thorpe trans.), 1966

Introduction to the Use of the Public Records, An, V. H. Galbraith, 1934

Itinerary in England and Wales in or about the Years 1535–1543, John Leland (L. T. Smith ed.), 5 vols., 1964

King John, W. L. Warren, 1961

Language and History in Early Britain, K. Jackson, 1953

Late Tudor and Early Stuart Geography, E. G. R. Taylor, 1934, Appendix of MSS and Printed Books

Laws of the Earliest English Kings, The, F. L. Attenborough (ed.), 1922

Lost Villages of England, The, M. Beresford, 1954

Making of Domesday Book, The, V. H. Galbraith, 1961

Medieval England: an aerial survey, M. Beresford and J. K. S. St Joseph, 1958

Medieval Foundations of England, The, G. O. Sayles, 1964

Methods of Chronology, A. E. Stamp, 1933

Monastic Order in England, The, D. Knowles, 2nd edn, 1966

Monasticon Anglicanum, William Dugdale (J. Caley, H. Ellis, B. Bandinel eds.), 1817–30

Monumental Brasses, J. Mann, 1957

Names of Towns and Cities in Britain, The, W. F. H. Nicolaisen, Margaret Gelling and Melville Richards, 1970

New Towns of the Middle Ages: Town Plantations in England, Wales and Gascony, M. Beresford, 1967

Norman Conquest, The, E. A. Freeman, 6 vols., 1867–79

Norman Conquest, The: Its Setting and Impact, D. Whitelock et al., 1966: 'The Anglo-Saxon Achievement', D. Whitelock; 'The Campaign of 1066', C. H. Lemmon; 'The Effects of the Norman Conquest', F. Barlow; 'William the Conqueror: Duke and King', D. C. Douglas

Normans and the Norman Conquest, The, R. A. Brown, 1969

Old Towns of England, The, C. Rouse, 2nd edn, 1943–4

On Britain and Germany (The Agricola and the Germania), Tacitus (H. Mattingly trans.), 1948

Opera, Simeon of Durham (T. Arnold ed.), 2 vols., 1882, 1885

Ordnance Survey
   Map of Britain in the Dark Ages, 2nd edn, 1954
   Map of Monastic Britain, South Sheet, 2nd edn, 1954
   Map of Roman Britain, 3rd edn, 1956
   Map of Southern Britain in the Iron Age, 1967

Origin of English Place-Names, The, P. H. Reaney, 1960

Origin of the English Nation, The, H. M. Chadwick, 1924

Oxford Companion to English Literature (especially the 'Perpetual Calendar' with English Regnal Years), P. Harvey, 3rd edn, 1936, p. 909f.

Oxford Dictionary of English Etymology, The, C. T. Onions (ed.), 1966

Oxford History of England, G. Clark (ed.), Vol. I: *Roman Britain and the English Settlements*, R. G. Collingwood and J. N. L. Myres, 2nd edn, 1937 – Vol. II: *Anglo-Saxon England*, F. M. Stenton, 1943 – Vol. III: *From Domesday Book to Magna Carta, 1087–1216*, A. L. Poole, 2nd edn, 1955 – Vol. IV: *The Thirteenth Century, 1216–1307*, M. Powicke, 2nd edn, 1962 – Vol.

v: *The Fourteenth Century, 1307–99*, M. McKisack, 1959 – Vol. VI: *The Fifteenth Century, 1399–1485*, E. F. Jacob, 1961 – Vol. VII: *The Earlier Tudors, 1485–1558*, J. D. Mackie, 1952

Parker Chronicle (832–900), The, A. H. Smith, 2nd edn, 1939

Parker Chronicle and Laws, The, R. Flower and A. H. Smith, 1941

Penguin Dictionary of Surnames, The, B. Cottle, 1967

Perambulation of Kent, A, W. Lambarde, 1570, edn of 1826, rep. 1970

Personality of Britain, The, C. Fox, 4th edn, 1943

Polychronicon, Ranulf Higden (C. Babington and J. R. Lumbry eds.), 9 vols., 1865f.

Pre-Feudal England: The Jutes, J. E. A. Jolliffe, 1933

Prehistoric Communities of the British Isles, V. G. Childe, 3rd edn, 1949

Printed Book, The, H. G. Aldis, 2nd edn, 1947

Roman Britain (Britain in Pictures), I. A. Richmond, 1947

Roman Britain, I. A. Richmond, 1955

Roman Forts of the Saxon Shore, The (H.M.S.O.), L. Cottrell, 1954

Roman Roads in Britain, Vol. I, I. D. Margary, 1955

Roman Silchester, G. C. Boon, 1958

Roman Ways in the Weald, I. D. Margary, 1948

Romans, Kelts and Saxons in Ancient Britain, R. E. Zachrisson, 1927

Scribes and Scholars, L. D. Reynolds and N. G. Wilson, 1968

Select Charters . . ., W. Stubbs (ed.), 8th edn, 1905

South-East England: Ancient Peoples and Places, R. F. Jessup, 1970

Studies in Chronology and History, R. L. Poole, 1934

Survey Gazetteer of the British Isles, The, J. Bartholomew (ed.), 9th edn, 1943

Survey of London, 1598, John Stow (H. B. Wheatley ed.), 1912

Tour through the Whole Island of Great Britain, A, D. Defoe, 2 vols., revised edn, 1962

Town and Country in Roman Britain, A. L. F. Rivet, 2nd edn, 1964

Tudor Geography, E. G. R. Taylor, 1930, Appendix I

Twelve Caesars, The, Suetonius (R. Graves trans.), 1957

Two of the Saxon Chronicles Parallel, C. Plummer (ed.), 2 vols., 1892, 1899

Venerabilis Baedae Opera Historica, C. Plummer (ed.), 2 vols., 1896

Wandering Scholars, The, H. Waddell, 6th edn, 1932

Weald, The, S. W. Wooldridge and F. Golding, 1953

Woodlands and Marshlands of England, The, H. A. Wilcox, 1933

INDEX OF PLACES

National Grid numbers in Italic

SURREY

Alfoldean *117330*, 10 n.58

Battersea *268769*, 22
Baynard's Park *086368*, 5 n.35
Beddington *297653*, 19
Bensbury, Wimbledon *224710*, 20 n.41, 21
Betchworth Castle *190501*, 12
Bletchingley *330510*, 11 n.62
Bourne, river *c.360560* etc., 19
Box Hill *180515*, 13 n.82

Carshalton *280643*, 17 n.19, 18
Catteshull Manor *986439*, 4
Cheam *242639*, 17 n.16
Chertsey *040670*, 2
Coway Stakes, 8
Croydon *320655*, 18 nn. 25f., 19, 25 n.c
Cuddington *c.228632*, 16 n.12, 18

Effingham *120540*, 12

Farnham *840470*, 3

Gatton *275530*, 5 n.30, 11
Godalming *965435*, 4
Guildford *995495*, 4 n.29, 5f., 21
Guildown Saxon Cemetery *988488*, 7

Haling *c.325645*, 19
Holmesdale – 2, 11

Kennington Palace *312781*, 22, 25 n.96
Kingston *180690*, 13f.

Lagham Manor *363480*, 23
Lambeth Palace *305791*, 22f.
Leatherhead *170560*, 13

Lingfield Church *390440*, 23 n.66
Loseley House *975472*, 4 n.25, 5

Merton *260700*, 18
Mole, river *130650* etc., 10
Molesey *145680*, 10 n.57, 13

Newark Priory *043577*, 7 n.47
Nonsuch Palace *228631* etc., 16 n.11, 18
Noviomagus – 21, 22

Oatlands Palace *c.085652*, 7
Ockham *070565*, 7, 11 n.61
Ockley *147397*, 10
Overy – 2 n.8

Pyrford *040583*, 7

Reigate *250500*, 11, 24 n.78
Richmond Palace *177748*, 14, 15

St. Catherine's Hill, Guildford *994483*, 5 n.35
Sheen *180745*, 14, 15
Southwark *320800*, 23
Stane Street – 10, 11 n.59
Starborough Castle *425441*, 23
Sutton Place *012537*, 7

Waddon *c.310650*, 19 n.33
Wandle, river – 17 n.19, 18, 19, 22
Wandsworth *255745*, 10 n.57, 22
Waverley Abbey *868453*, 4, 5 n.33
Wey, river – 4, 7
White Hill (or Downs) *120494*, 13
Wimbledon *245715*, 20
Woking Old Hall *030570*, 7
Woodcote *c.290610*, 21

SUSSEX

Amberley Castle (W. Sx) *027132*, 35
Appledram (W. Sx) *840030*, 34
Arun, river *020120*, 35 n.69, 36

Arundel (Forest) (W. Sx) *015070*, 30, 36f., 66
Ashburnham (E. Sx) *690145*, 30 n.15, 58
Ashdown Forest (E. Sx) *c.460300*, 66